Cases in Health Care Marketing

John L. Fortenberry, Jr., MBA, PhD, PhD

Chair, James K. Elrod Department of Health Administration
MHA Program Director
James K. Elrod Professor of Health Administration
Professor of Marketing
School of Business Administration
LSU Shreveport
Shreveport, Louisiana

JONES AND BARTLETT PUBLISHERS
Sudbury, Massachusetts
BOSTON   TORONTO   LONDON   SINGAPORE

World Headquarters

Jones and Bartlett Publishers
40 Tall Pine Drive
Sudbury, MA 01776
978-443-5000
info@jbpub.com
www.jbpub.com

Jones and Bartlett Publishers
Canada
6339 Ormindale Way
Mississauga, Ontario L5V 1J2
Canada

Jones and Bartlett Publishers
International
Barb House, Barb Mews
London W6 7PA
United Kingdom

Jones and Bartlett's books and products are available through most bookstores and online booksellers. To contact Jones and Bartlett Publishers directly, call 800-832-0034, fax 978-443-8000, or visit our website, www.jbpub.com.

Substantial discounts on bulk quantities of Jones and Bartlett's publications are available to corporations, professional associations, and other qualified organizations. For details and specific discount information, contact the special sales department at Jones and Bartlett via the above contact information or send an email to specialsales@jbpub.com.

This publication is designed to provide accurate and authoritative information in regard to the Subject Matter covered. It is sold with the understanding that the publisher is not engaged in rendering legal, accounting, or other professional service. If legal advice or other expert assistance is required, the service of a competent professional person should be sought.

Production Credits
Publisher: Michael Brown
Editorial Assistant: Catie Heverling
Editorial Assistant: Teresa Reilly
Production Manager: Tracey Chapman
Senior Marketing Manager: Sophie Fleck
Manufacturing and Inventory Control Supervisor: Amy Bacus
Composition: DSCS/Absolute Service, Inc.
Cover Design: Kristin E. Parker
Cover Image: © Petrosg/Dreamstime.com
Printing and Binding: Malloy, Inc.
Cover Printing: Malloy, Inc.

Library of Congress Cataloging-in-Publication Data
Fortenberry, John L.
   Cases in health care marketing / John L. Fortenberry Jr.
       p. ; cm.
   Includes bibliographical references and index.
   ISBN-13: 978-0-7637-6448-7 (pbk.)
   ISBN-10: 0-7637-6448-5 (pbk.)
   1. Medical care—United States—Marketing—Case studies. 2. Medical care—Needs assessment—United States—Case studies. I. Title.
   [DNLM: 1. Marketing of Health Services—United States—Case Reports. 2. Health Services Needs and Demand—economics—United States—Case Reports. W 74 F737c 2011]
   RA410.56.F67 2011
   362.1068'8—dc22
                              2009039384
6048

Printed in the United States of America
14 13 12 11 10   10 9 8 7 6 5 4 3 2 1

Dedicated to my mother, Mary Margaret;
my sister, Lisa; and my brother, Parrish

Acknowledgments

Cases in Health Care Marketing represents my fifth book and second published by Jones and Bartlett Publishers. This particular work proved very challenging as it forced me to draw on significantly more creativity than that required by traditional marketing textbooks and journal articles. It seemed simple at the onset. I just needed to reduce to writing around 40 of the countless marketing scenarios that I present in my classes every semester in order to assist students in their understanding of given topics. However, as I went about converting 5-minute oral presentations of scenarios from my marketing classes into 1500-word written passages of the same, it quickly became apparent to me that this would be much more difficult than I ever could have imagined.

Questions came from every angle. Of the countless scenarios conveyed in my classes, which should I present in this work? How much or how little detail should I include in each scenario? Should the characters in cases resolve their given dilemmas or should I leave that to the reader? Slowly but surely, I answered these questions and each of the 40 cases presented in this work began to take shape.

At times, I felt more like a playwright than an academic author as I went about creating storylines, crafting plots, and generating characters and their associated personas. Indeed, the writing style required of this work is far removed from anything that I have ever written in my academic career. But despite the associated challenges, this was perhaps my most rewarding writing experience and I believe that the finished product will do more to educate and enlighten readers than anything that I have previously written.

Of course, this work would not have been possible without the assistance of Michael Brown, Catie Heverling, Sophie Fleck, Tracey Chapman, and the rest of the Jones and Bartlett team who provided excellent guidance and support throughout the development, publication, and promotion of this text. Furthermore, for their support of my scholarly writing efforts, I must thank several administrators at LSU Shreveport, namely, Drs. Vincent J. Marsala (Chancellor), Paul Sisson (Vice Chancellor for Academic Affairs), David Gustavson (Dean of the College of Business, Education, and Human Development), and Douglas S. Bible (Associate Dean of the College of Business, Education, and Human Development). Finally, James K. Elrod, President and Chief Executive Officer of Willis-Knighton Health System, deserves to be recognized for his ongoing support of my scholarly writing endeavors.

I am deeply appreciative of the guidance and support offered by the individuals noted above. They each have played an important role in helping me author *Cases in Health Care Marketing*.

About the Author

John L. Fortenberry, Jr. serves as Chair of the James K. Elrod Department of Health Administration, MHA Program Director, James K. Elrod Professor of Health Administration, and Professor of Marketing in the School of Business Administration at LSU Shreveport where he teaches a variety of courses in both health administration and marketing.

He received a BBA in Marketing from the University of Mississippi; an MBA from Mississippi College; a PhD in Public Administration and Public Policy, with concentrations in Health Administration, Human Resource Management, and Organization Theory, from Auburn University; and a PhD in Business Administration, with a major in Marketing, from the University of Manchester in the United Kingdom.

Dr. Fortenberry's academic research interests are centered on marketing, including the components of advertising, consumer behavior, and strategy. His specific sector interests include health, retail, and transportation industries. He is the author of five books, including *Health Care Marketing: Tools and Techniques,* published by Jones and Bartlett Publishers.

Contents

Preface

Cases present opportunities to learn a great deal about marketing issues, events, and circumstances occurring in and around healthcare institutions. The thought processes that they evoke are far greater than those provided by readings in standard healthcare marketing textbooks that merely identify and explain terms, practices, and procedures. Instead, cases force readers to think through myriad elements that have direct and indirect linkages with internal and external environments. Hence, they compel readers to apply the tools and techniques that are learned from standard marketing textbooks to resolve or otherwise address applicable dilemmas.

Further enhancing intellectual development, cases rarely have single, defined solutions, but instead may be successfully addressed in multiple fashions, depending on the nature and arrangement of associated remedies. All in all, cases are fantastic learning devices and possibly do more to prepare one to address real-world situations than anything other than direct experience. Given the value that cases provide readers, I authored *Cases in Health Care Marketing*.

Written for healthcare administrators, clinicians, students, and other interested parties, *Cases in Health Care Marketing* presents a series of 40 cases, partitioned into six categories; namely, product, brand, and identity management; marketing communications; marketing management; marketing strategy and planning; consumer behavior and target marketing; and environmental analysis and competitive assessment. Each case is placed in its own chapter and includes an introductory snapshot, which provides a quick outline of case components, including locations, characters, and contexts, permitting individuals and groups to more easily engage in associated discussions and debates without confusing the various elements of given cases. Discussion inquiries are provided at the conclusion of each chapter, providing challenging questions and associated directives to further bolster knowledge and insight. Additionally, a glossary is included at the conclusion of this work.

As for the specific topics addressed in this book, they are numerous and sufficiently differentiated from one another from chapter to chapter, but there are many common themes running through the entire collection of cases, recurring throughout the text to emphasize their associated importance. Frequent and inexcusable oversights, such as failing to monitor the environment, taking the patronage of customers for granted, sinking into complacency when all is well, deploying marketing communications without measuring performance, and operating marketing departments that fail to deliver across every component of the discipline are brought front and center across the pages of this text. In some cases, conflict exists between parties, with individuals disagreeing on the manner in which to address certain situations. In other cases, individuals are presented with personal and professional quandaries, not knowing the appropriate direction to take when faced with given problems or circumstances. Readers are charged with making sense of things and determining prudent courses of action.

Each case presented in this work is fictitious. The locations, institutions, and characters have all been derived from my imagination. The storylines, too, are the product of my imagination; however, they each have been influenced by actual events that I have been exposed to over the course of my career. The scenarios presented herein can and do actually occur in the healthcare industry. Of course, any resemblance noted between the cases and actual persons or places is unintentional and purely coincidental.

It is perhaps most beneficial to use *Cases in Health Care Marketing* as a supplemental work alongside a standard healthcare marketing textbook, such as my own *Health Care Marketing: Tools and Techniques* or perhaps Eric Berkowitz's *Essentials of Health Care Marketing*, both of which are published by Jones and Bartlett Publishers. This tandem approach permits readers to learn and refer to theoretical and practical facets of the discipline of marketing, courtesy of the standard healthcare marketing textbook, and then exercise their skills at deployment, courtesy of this particular book.

Whether using this text as the basis for discussions and debates within classrooms, executive offices, or other venues, I anticipate that the end result will be education and enlightenment that will make readers more proficient marketers and more capable healthcare executives.

It is my hope that this text advances your administrative skill set and permits you to see what others cannot.

John L. Fortenberry, Jr.

PART ONE

Product, Brand, and Identity Management

CHAPTER 1

Setting the Stage

SNAPSHOT

Institution:
Meadowbrook Clinic, a two-physician medical practice specializing in family medicine

Location:
Washington (population 438,042), located in the East South Central region of the United States

Characters:
Ms. Linda Douglas, Administrator (retiring)
Mr. James Reynolds, Administrator (newly hired)
Dr. Karen Robinson, Co-Owner and Physician
Dr. Thomas White, Co-Owner and Physician
(all of Meadowbrook Clinic)

Context:
In this case, a newly hired administrator seeks to professionalize the business operations of a clinic, but shortly after orientation, he sees conflict between a key goal of its physician owners and reality.

James Reynolds is excited. He just received the telephone call that he had been waiting for—an opportunity to join Meadowbrook Clinic as its new administrator. Accepting this new opportunity, James is especially enthusiastic because he will be the first professional administrator in the history of the medical practice. While this new employment position will likely prove to be challenging, it will afford him a unique opportunity to professionalize operations; something James welcomes.

Owned by Drs. Karen Robinson and Thomas White, Meadowbrook Clinic specializes in family medicine. The two-physician practice has grown over its 6 years of existence, bringing the clinic to a point where professional administrative practices are needed to enhance internal and external business operations, affording greater opportunities for prosperity. Drs. Robinson and White were beginning to see weaknesses resulting from inefficient operations that were negatively impacting practice growth. This they attributed to a lack of vision and expertise on the part of the clinic's office Administrator, Linda Douglas.

Drs. Robinson and White have been very proud of their practice's fast-paced growth over its brief lifespan, but they are hungry for more. The clinic is situated in the East South Central region of the United States, specifically, the city of Washington (population 438,042), an area that is expected to witness enhanced population growth in coming years. The two physicians wish to position their practice to capitalize on the coming boom. Drs. Robinson and White were especially desirous of engaging in marketing to increase patient traffic, perhaps positioning the practice to hire another physician to address the extra volume. Unfortunately, Linda did not possess the skill set to capitalize on coming opportunities, nor did she have the desire to acquire the skills to do so.

Not unlike many small medical practices, the administrative infrastructure of Meadowbrook Clinic merely had evolved, primarily as a clerical function at the hands of Linda, who possessed solid office management skills but lacked formal training in executive administration. Her formal education was limited to high school and some coursework in the area of office management at a technical college; most of her training was on-the-job. Linda had performed well in past years, but the business of medicine and the intricacies of the external environment were growing increasingly complex, convincing Drs. Robinson and White that a professionally trained administrator was necessary.

For the medical practice, the timing could not have been better. Linda was preparing to retire, making for an easy and conflict-free transition to professional management. To ease the transition even further, Linda agreed, at the request of Drs. Robinson and White, to remain employed until Meadowbrook Clinic had successfully recruited a new administrator. With James' hire, Linda's retirement could now proceed, prefaced by a brief orientation period that she would provide for James.

James indeed fit the role of the professional healthcare administrator. He possessed 15 years of experience in ambulatory care management, primarily working for for-profit and not-for-profit hospital-based clinics. He also held a Master of Health Administration degree and a few administrative certifications, affording additional knowledge and providing further confirmations of his abilities to enhance operations at Meadowbrook Clinic.

Presenting for work on his first day, James was warmly welcomed by all of Meadowbrook Clinic's employees. A 2-week orientation period conducted by Linda immediately ensued, permitting James an invaluable opportunity to observe current practices, shadowing the very person who had been in charge of such for years. This also facilitated James' plan to simply observe clinic activities for 2 weeks, upon which he would provide a preliminary report to Drs. Robinson and White outlining his observations and plans for improving administrative operations.

Nearly 2 weeks into his observations, James, for the most part, had come to understand Meadowbrook Clinic. He witnessed good things that he believed should be retained and bad things that he definitely was determined to eliminate. As for the good things, he noted a high degree of camaraderie among professional, technical, and clerical staff members, making for a cordial atmosphere that positively resonated with Meadowbrook Clinic's patients. Further, maintaining adequate personnel coverage across the clinic's schedule (weekdays from 8 AM to 6 PM) was problem free, with employees working closely with each other to ensure that Meadowbrook's patient base was efficiently and effectively addressed.

James also noted an excellent physical environment, with the clinic sporting an attractive, comfortable decor that was aesthetically and ergonomically pleasing for both patients and employees. Basic administrative processes seemed to be in order, with admissions, payroll, and other core activities being carried out prudently. Further, patients seemed very pleased with both the care delivered at the clinic and ancillary administrative processes, although satisfaction was not being formally measured.

James indeed believed that Meadowbrook Clinic possessed a firm foundation upon which future gains could be accomplished. However, to do so, he knew that a number of weaknesses would need to be addressed. The administrative framework, for example, was very visibly a clerical model, with Linda serving primarily as an advanced paper-pusher. Executive management processes and practices were universally absent, just as James expected. No efforts were made in the areas of strategic planning, with the clinic not even having a mission statement. Also absent were any stated goals and objectives, hampering opportunities to engage in organized pursuits and track progress.

Marketing efforts were nonexistent, with Meadowbrook Clinic relying completely on word-of-mouth communications from satisfied patients and referrals from other practitioners in the marketplace for new patient traffic. Nor were there any efforts to monitor the environment or track patient satisfaction. As James had expected, the basic office management requirements of the medical practice were being handily addressed, but advanced administrative techniques and procedures were absent.

James was confident that he could design and implement an administrative floor plan that would set the stage for professional business operations. But he was particularly concerned regarding one of the key desirables expressed by Drs. Robinson and White—growth. James knew that he could develop a marketing communications plan that would bolster patient volume, but he was unsure of exactly how the clinic would accommodate that growth.

By his estimation, Meadowbrook Clinic's waiting room and parking area were reaching their capacity limitations with the current patient volume addressed by the practice. Further, the clinic was landlocked, completely surrounded by other establishments, with no easy opportunities to purchase adjacent space for clinic and parking area enhancements. Drs. Robinson and White had indicated their satisfaction with the location of Meadowbrook Clinic and had even invested thousands of dollars recently to upgrade the medical practice. These were clear indications that the two physicians had no intentions of accommodating growth through the physical relocation of Meadowbrook Clinic.

As James' 2-week observation period drew to a close, he entered the weekend with the goal of writing a report conveying recommendations to Drs. Robinson and White. Some concerns could easily be addressed; others would be more difficult.

DISCUSSION

1. James indicated that he planned to install an administrative floor plan to set the stage for professional administrative operations. Although the case gives a few indications of what he has in mind, think about strategic management, marketing, and other professional management activities, and provide insights into exactly what such a floor plan would involve.

2. Based on accounts by Drs. Robinson and White, Meadowbrook Clinic seems to have witnessed pleasing growth over its 6-year history, but it now seems that growth limitations are appearing, which the two physicians attribute to a lack of skill and innovation on the part of Linda. Based on James' findings concerning growth barriers, do you think Drs. Robinson and White correctly identified the cause of plateauing practice growth? Please justify your response.

3. Assume that the physical environment of Meadowbrook Clinic and its parking area are of sufficient size to accommodate increased patient volume. How would this change your response provided in the prior discussion inquiry? Be sure to provide descriptive details.

4. Assume that James is accurate in his assessment of the physical growth barriers faced by Meadowbrook Clinic. Assume also that Drs. Robinson and White will not consider relocating their medical practice for the purpose of increasing capacity. Given all of this, what, if any, avenues of practice growth remain possible?

5. What do you believe would enter a potential patient's mind if he or she drove to a clinic and witnessed a jam-packed parking area and waiting room, clearly demonstrating that the clinic was operating at or even beyond capacity? What effect would this have on growth? What are the implications of this for marketing?

2

Shoring Up the Servicescape

SNAPSHOT

Institution:
Grace Hospital, a 425-bed, not-for-profit hospital providing general medical and surgical services

Location:
Richmond (population 175,710), located in the West South Central region of the United States

Characters:
Mr. Todd Davis, President and Chief Executive Officer
Ms. Maria Stevens, Vice President of Nursing
Mr. Bradley Walters, Vice President of Marketing
(all of Grace Hospital)

Context:
In this case, a nursing executive improves the physical environment of the areas falling under her supervision and responsibility, but encounters difficulties when trying to effect the same improvements in areas falling outside of her span of control.

Making her rounds at the beginning of the day's work, Maria Stevens cannot help to be anything but frustrated. She has been employed as Vice President of Nursing at Grace Hospital for 5 years and has witnessed the best of patient care and attention delivered by its employees. But all of that excellence is tarnished by weaknesses in other areas of the hospital, which cloud what otherwise would be a beautiful picture. Completing her initial rounds of the day, she makes up her mind that now is the time to address these weaknesses that hamper across-the-board excellence at Grace Hospital.

The biggest issue, as Maria sees it, is that the quality of the physical plant, fixtures, and furnishings of Grace Hospital is not consistent with the quality delivered by its caregivers. As for the physical plant, the hospital has very obvious shortcomings: chipped paint on the walls, cracked tile on the floors, blotched ceiling tiles evidencing apparent leaks, and color schemes throughout the institution that are very much outdated. Patient waiting areas have mismatched furniture, some of it damaged by the normal wear and tear of public use and, at least in some cases, outright abuse. Further, landscaping around the hospital could be much improved with even the slightest bit of attention that quite obviously has not been forwarded. On top of that, the parking areas are patchwork quilts of concrete and asphalt with an occasional blade of grass bursting through crevices; segments pieced together over the years and hastily repaired only when absolutely necessary, with little concern for aesthetics or even functionality. Maria believed that if as much attention was given to these areas as was given to patient care, Grace Hospital would rise to new levels in the minds of its customers and the surrounding community.

Grace Hospital, a financially sound, 425-bed, not-for-profit medical facility, is located in Richmond, a city of 175,710 located in the West South Central region of the United States. It was constructed 50 years ago and periodically has been upgraded, with the last comprehensive refurbishment occurring 15 years ago. Since that time, only routine maintenance has occurred, with many oversights taking place along the way. The hospital grounds, however, have never been addressed professionally, just simple lawn care—plenty of opportunities for improvement, but none ever taken.

Having recently constructed and landscaped a new home, Maria well knows the costs of construction and comprehensive refurbishment and refinement, but she does not believe that such drastic measures are warranted at Grace Hospital. In her opinion, the primary issues of concern simply call for more attention to detail. The repairs and minor enhancements that Maria believes would improve the aesthetics and ambiance of Grace Hospital's servicescape would not call for terribly significant resources.

She estimates that, apart from minor material expenses, the only additional requirement would involve the time and attention of maintenance personnel and perhaps also those in environmental services—individuals who are already employed by Grace Hospital. Given this, the most obvious challenge to achieving Maria's vision of improved property, plant, and equipment is the direction of attention to aesthetics and ambiance by Grace Hospital's administration and associated departments, namely maintenance and environmental services.

Maria indeed knows the power of aesthetics and ambiance. When she was hired as Grace Hospital's Vice President of Nursing, she was appalled that clinical staff members, regardless of job title or department, were wearing scrubs of every color in the rainbow, confusing patients and visitors and even creating difficulties for the staff members themselves. Order was needed, so she instituted a policy that involved assigning scrub colors to given departments, giving associated members a uniform appearance that fostered identification and professionalism. Strict grooming protocols were instituted and enforced to ensure that employees looked their best as they went about conducting their various duties and responsibilities. These simple changes elevated the appearance of clinical employees by leaps and bounds, creating order from what once appeared to be massive chaos.

Maria did not stop there. She then focused on reducing noise levels throughout patient care areas, knowing that excessive noise negatively impacted patient comfort. One of the biggest culprits, the overhead paging system, was eliminated, being replaced by cell phones assigned to each employee, greatly reducing noise throughout the hospital. Doors were adjusted so they would not slam, hospital carts were modified to minimize noise, and foam padding was added on various surfaces, such as pneumatic tube and patient chart receptacles, to reduce clanging. Sound monitoring devices were mounted at nurse stations, providing visual indications of ambient noise levels, which reminded employees to take steps to be as quiet as possible. These efforts resulted in a vastly improved environment, for both employees and patients, garnering Maria much praise throughout the hospital.

With her sights now set on aesthetic and ambiance matters resting in areas beyond her formal scope of authority, Maria needs to formulate a plan for approaching Todd Davis, Grace Hospital's President and Chief Executive Officer, in hopes that he will agree with her assessment of the state of the institution's environment and authorize improvements. As her ideas ultimately will yield a more marketable hospital, she decides to first meet with her fellow senior manager, Bradley Walters, who serves as Grace Hospital's Vice President of Marketing.

Excited about the opportunities for improvement, Maria shared her vision with Bradley, who indicated that her ideas were most pleasing to hear. He communicated that he completely agreed with her assessment, noting that for years, he had viewed the lack of attention to detail to limit Grace Hospital's ultimate potential as an institution. This, Bradley expressed, even limited the appeals that Grace Hospital could use in its various marketing communications campaigns. Maria's initial excitement, though, turned to disappointment when Bradley informed her that he had made countless efforts in recent months and years to initiate improvements, but that his efforts always fell on deaf ears, with Todd refusing to act on his suggestions and recommendations.

Bradley explained that the resistance seemed to stem from Todd's view that the recommended improvements constituted costs, rather than investments, in Grace Hospital. He noted that Todd always responded that Grace Hospital was financially sound and was generating significant business and questioned why upgrades were even necessary. Providing even further detail, Bradley went on to state that, based on interactions with Todd, who has served as Grace Hospital's President and Chief Executive Officer for just over 2 years, he viewed him to be a "status quo" executive, noting that eventually this attitude would catch up with Grace Hospital, likely costing the institution dearly. Maria responded that the neglected physical plant likely was already taking a toll on the hospital.

Not one to easily concede, Maria suggested to Bradley that they work together to develop and assemble an economical plan for initiating improvements. If Todd viewed improvements simply to be costs, then an inexpensive plan might be just enough to persuade him to authorize the improvements. Perhaps Grace Hospital could even call upon volunteers who would contribute their time and talents to improve the facility. Mutually excited, the pair agreed to meet the following morning to begin brainstorming on the many possibilities, with confidence that Grace Hospital would soon receive much needed refinements.

DISCUSSION

1. Grace Hospital seems to possess servicescape excellence in nursing service, but not in other important areas of the facility; something Maria sought to correct due to associated negative consequences. Think deeply on the aesthetics and ambiance of the servicescapes of healthcare institutions and prepare a list of negative effects that occur when servicescapes are inferior. Identify the parties that inferior servicescapes impact and describe how such environments impact each party.

2. Bradley mentioned to Maria that Grace Hospital's servicescape weaknesses limited the appeals that the hospital could use in its various marketing communications campaigns. Based on your knowledge of marketing and marketing communications, what did Bradley mean by this statement?

3. Todd's mindset that a financially sound and full hospital need not invest in improvements is unfortunately not uncommon among some in the healthcare industry. Why do you believe that individuals would possess such a mindset? What would you envision their career paths to be?

4. Given Todd's history of resistance to improvements, Maria and Bradley decided to strive for change by developing an economical plan for enhancing Grace Hospital, even suggesting the possibility of calling on volunteers for contributions. Based on the weaknesses noted by Maria, develop a cost-effective plan of improvement by identifying possible "fixes" that could be implemented in a manner that would likely be acceptable to Todd.

5. Assume that Todd rejects the economical improvement plan formulated by Maria and Bradley. Given that the consequences of failing to make improvements might cause real harm to Grace Hospital, what action, if any, should the two take? Please justify your response.

Revitalizing a Brand

SNAPSHOT

Institution:
Plaza Home Health Services, a recently established home health agency

Location:
Georgetown (population 45,857), located in the West North Central region of the United States

Characters:
Ms. Nancy Edwards, Co-Owner and Nurse
Ms. Jennifer Moore, Co-Owner and Nurse
(both of Plaza Home Health Services)

Context:
In this case, two entrepreneurs establish a home health agency and quickly encounter overwhelming success, giving them the opportunity to rethink some hastily made branding decisions.

Nancy Edwards and Jennifer Moore, co-owners of Plaza Home Health Services, are celebrating their 1-year anniversary as healthcare entrepreneurs and, at this juncture, have decided to invest in some much needed identity enhancements for their company. Specifically, the two entrepreneurs are seeking to elevate the status and stature of Plaza Home Health Services by upgrading its associated brand image, bolstering corporate identity and consumer recognition in an effort to position the firm for continued success in coming years.

Plaza Home Health Services was established rather hurriedly 1 year ago by Nancy and Jennifer. The two were employed as staff nurses at a medical center in Georgetown, a city of 45,857 located in the West North Central region of the United States, and saw an opportunity to capitalize on the growing demand for home health services in the marketplace. In their informal marketing research endeavors, Nancy and Jennifer witnessed unrestrained enthusiasm for their proposed business, so much so that they decided to fast-track its development and rollout.

Despite this rush to commercialization, Plaza Home Health Services' results have been nothing less than stellar, with the company quickly assuming the market leadership position amidst a pool of three very established and highly competitive home health service providers in Georgetown. Pleased with their good fortune, Nancy and Jennifer attribute the success of their business to their commitment to deliver home health service excellence in a comprehensive fashion, taking great pains to exceed the expectations of customers and eclipse the service levels offered by rivals in the market.

As home health agencies deliver services remotely, the two entrepreneurs had a thorough understanding that their caregivers must be top quality, leading them to assemble a compensation and benefits package that permitted them to recruit the most capable personnel in the market, creating a key competitive advantage. Further, they ensured that Plaza Home Health Services' policies addressed every facet of business operation and service delivery. Providers, for example, followed strict protocols on everything from grooming and attire to professional courtesy and patient care delivery.

Plaza Home Health Services is financially viable and, thanks to the discipline of Nancy and Jennifer, has acquired significant cash reserves for future growth. One year on, Plaza Home Health Services indeed presents a very different financial picture than that witnessed when Nancy and Jennifer initiated the venture. Like many small business entrepreneurs, the two had only a small amount of personal savings to draw on as they launched their company. Their rush to market, together with insufficient cash reserves, forced Nancy and Jennifer to make some identity compromises which they now seek to upgrade, enhance, and repair, courtesy of the receipt of business success and proper funding.

The compromises in identity were numerous, but they each centered around one thing—Plaza Home Health Services' poorly conceived logo. This, in turn, resulted in aesthetically displeasing and uninspiring business cards, promotional brochures, and building signage, as each incorporated the establishment's logo. Indeed, one could question whether the agency even has a logo, as the only visualization is simply the text "Plaza Home Health Services" in the bold, italic version of the Times New Roman font. This simple brand display is used, in black, on both Plaza Home Health Services' office building and on its roadside signage. It also is used in all of the company's sales literature, with each piece being laser-printed with black toner. Even the company's business cards are laser-printed, using perforated sheets of paper which are then separated to form individual cards.

All in all, the appearance of every branding element associated with Plaza Home Health Services is very amateurish; a necessity at one time, but no longer needed thanks to business success and resulting cash flow. The time has finally come for Nancy and Jennifer to craft a plan to upgrade the elements of identity associated with their company.

Meeting to discuss improvements, Nancy and Jennifer made the decision to first review a variety of branding considerations in the context of the company's current image and associated brand attributes. From this discussion, the two entrepreneurs indicated high satisfaction with the brand name of their operation and they agreed that no changes were necessary, especially as this would create confusion among their customers who already had grown very familiar with the Plaza Home Health Services brand name. They next turned their attention to the components of the logo, including its text, symbols, and color or colors to be used.

As for the components of Plaza Home Health Services' logo, Nancy and Jennifer indicated a desire to incorporate both text and symbol components to identify the company, as they believed that this served to better attract attention and facilitate recognition. Given that their current text design used one of the most common fonts, the two preferred something that was a bit more exotic. In order to identify preferences, Nancy and Jennifer looked through several font books and came to realize a preference for sans serif as opposed to serif fonts. Making a short list of possibilities, Nancy and Jennifer decided to delay their ultimate selection, as they wanted to experiment with variations using a graphics software package.

As for the symbol, Nancy and Jennifer found this to be especially challenging, as the three competitors in the marketplace were already using perhaps the most common medical symbols—the hospital cross, the medical caduceus, and the pulse trace—leaving the two entrepreneurs at a major loss for something relevant but also unique. After some debate, though, Nancy and Jennifer decided that they easily could look to variants of these symbols. This would permit them to incorporate classic symbolism into their logo, but do so in a manner that would enhance brand identity, as the ultimate design would possess a unique creative treatment. Having made good progress in this area, Nancy and Jennifer decided to table their discussion on symbols pending a review of clip art catalogs to examine symbol variants, although they also indicated that they would be interested in adding nurse images to the list of symbol possibilities for consideration.

As for the color or colors used by Plaza Home Health Services, Nancy and Jennifer definitely were interested in leaving black behind, as they have exclusively been using this by default, courtesy of their monochrome laser printer. Of the three other home health operations in Georgetown, Nancy and Jennifer were very aware that the colors of red, blue, and green were already being used. To eliminate the possibility of confusion in the marketplace, Nancy and Jennifer agreed that they should avoid these colors or close variants, as they plan to use color to help differentiate their home health operation from others. On their color short list, they decided to include purple, gold, and orange, with both entrepreneurs agreeing to give the ultimate selection some thought in coming days to ensure that the selection proved fitting for the establishment. They also agreed that Plaza Home Health Services should use a single color for their logo, as multiple colors, at least in some cases, can increase the costs of printing.

Nancy and Jennifer were pleased with their first steps toward improving the brand identity of Plaza Home Health Services. In coming days, they planned to further investigate their various text, image, and color options and then work to sketch a design combining the items to form a rudimentary logo. They then planned to submit this rough illustration to an area graphic designer, who they would look to for the purpose of professionalizing the image, perfecting the artwork for inclusion across the range of Plaza Home Health Services' various marketing communications.

DISCUSSION

1. For an entire year, Nancy and Jennifer marketed their home health service using very primitive forms of identity. They were very fortunate that clients looked beyond the firm's marketing communications in deciding to extend patronage. Place yourself in the role of a potential client receiving business cards and brochures like those distributed on behalf of Plaza Home Health Services. What thoughts would go through your mind?

2. Nancy and Jennifer have made a wise decision to upgrade Plaza Home Health Services' elements of identity, with the establishment's business cards being slated, among other things, for improvement. How might business cards be even more important for establishments delivering offerings remotely, like home health agencies, than for establishments delivering offerings at a central location?

3. Based on your own preferences regarding color and design, create a mock-up of a business card for Plaza Home Health Services. Place your own name and contact information in the business card. Your business card must be sized in accordance with the designated standard for such in your area of the world (2" × 3.5" in the United States). While a hand-drawn sketch will suffice, a card designed using graphics software is preferred.

4. Nancy and Jennifer plan to use Plaza Home Health Services' revised logo in a number of communicative devices, including a promotional brochure. Aside from the logo itself, what other visual elements would you include in such a brochure? Be sure to give specifics regarding the various visual elements you would include, as well as your justification for using them in Plaza Home Health Services' brochure.

5. Nancy and Jennifer have indicated that they plan to upgrade Plaza Home Health Services' building signage. Is this necessary for businesses that provide services that are delivered remotely (i.e., at the customer's location rather than corporate headquarters)? Why or why not?

4

Expectations and Experiences

SNAPSHOT

Institutions:
Emerald Hills Medical Center, a 570-bed, not-for-profit medical center providing general medical and surgical services
Concord Marketing, a marketing consulting firm hired by Emerald Hills' Chief Executive Officer to provide marketing services on behalf of the medical center

Location:
Plymouth (population 671,588), located in the Mountain region of the United States

Characters:
Ms. Lisa Jackson, Chief Nursing Officer
Ms. Elizabeth Martin, Chief Executive Officer
Mr. Donald Williamson, former Chief Marketing Officer,
(*all of Emerald Hills Medical Center*)

Context:
In this case, a medical center's top nursing executive comes into conflict with the establishment's Chief Executive Officer, claiming that a unilaterally imposed advertising campaign oversells the medical center and sets patients up for disappointment.

Lisa Jackson, Chief Nursing Officer at Emerald Hills Medical Center, is troubled. Emerald Hills' new advertising campaign has just been launched and she is not at all pleased. Lisa's specific concerns are that the campaign does not accurately portray Emerald Hills Medical Center and will almost certainly set patients, their families, and visitors up for disappointment. This has huge implications for Lisa and her staff as their involvement in direct patient care places them on the front lines, positioning each of them to be the first to hear, and consequently address, patient and family frustrations and disappointments.

This all started several weeks ago when Lisa, a 25-year nursing veteran and long-time nurse executive at Emerald Hills, was asked, along with her fellow senior managers, to attend a meeting called by Emerald Hills' Chief Executive Officer, Elizabeth Martin. The purpose of the meeting was to discuss marketing at the 570-bed not-for-profit medical center. Lisa and the other senior managers at Emerald Hills were well aware that the medical center's long-time Chief Marketing Officer, Donald Williamson, had resigned from his post to assume a similar position elsewhere, but they were not aware of the latest—that Elizabeth was going to forgo hiring a replacement for Donald. Instead, Elizabeth communicated that Emerald Hills Medical Center would be outsourcing its marketing function to a consulting firm, Concord Marketing.

Elizabeth, who is new both to Emerald Hills and the Chief Executive Officer role, viewed this decision to be cost-conscious at a time when the economy of the region was especially poor, placing all businesses, including healthcare establishments, under financial pressure. Elizabeth believed that outsourcing would permit marketing operations to continue essentially unchanged while reducing associated costs. She also believed that the cost savings would help to better position Emerald Hills against its marketplace rivals, numbering five, as battles for market share waged on in the city of Plymouth (population 671,588), located in the Mountain region of the United States. After explaining her rationale for the decision, Elizabeth then presented a brief video profiling Concord Marketing, providing insights into the firm's capabilities and experience.

At the conclusion of the presentation, Elizabeth entertained questions from her senior management team. Perhaps the biggest concern expressed by the senior managers pertained to the ability of an off-site company to address comprehensively all of the marketing functions of Emerald Hills Medical Center. The video clearly illustrated Concord's ability to develop and implement advertising and direct mail campaigns, but that only focuses on the marketing communications component. It said nothing about marketing planning, public relations activities, patient satisfaction research, and so on—all things that Donald routinely engaged in as he led marketing operations.

Elizabeth responded that matters beyond marketing communications would be handled by her office, via the relocation of a marketing staffer from the soon-to-be former marketing department. Elizabeth further conveyed that she planned to retitle the position held by the staffer from Marketing Assistant to Community Relations Officer. The team remained skeptical of the plan, but Elizabeth's mind was made up and her plan was put into action shortly after their meeting.

Two weeks later, a team from Concord Marketing visited Emerald Hills Medical Center and, among other things, its members met individually with the medical center's senior managers in an effort to gain ideas and insights into how to best portray Emerald Hills in an upcoming marketing communications campaign. As did her fellow senior managers, Lisa shared her views on Emerald Hills, noting its points-of-parity and points-of-difference with competitors. After a day of interviews, the team from Concord then departed, noting that all insights, suggestions, and comments would be taken into account as they devised the upcoming campaign.

As the new month came in, so too did the new marketing communications campaign, with billboards posting around the city on Friday, accompanied by television and radio campaigns scheduled to begin on the same day. The senior management team had not been privileged to a preview of the campaign, nor had they been involved in its approval—that was done by Elizabeth—so each of them waited with great anticipation to see the end result.

On that Friday morning, the billboard posters were making their rounds early; so early, in fact, that Lisa was among the first to see a posted billboard, viewing a panel that happened to be placed on her route to work. As she approached the billboard, the Emerald Hills Medical Center's logo was clearly visible from a great distance—a good thing Lisa thought. Getting closer, the artwork, depicting a trio of clinicians happily staring back at the viewer, was very clear—another positive element Lisa believed. But the slogan "Medical care delivered in the most comfortable of settings" was troubling to her. Sure, Emerald Hills Medical Center was a comfortable environment, but it was not anything special; certainly nothing that could not be found at any of Emerald Hills' competitors. Yet, the billboard advertisement was conveying to patients and visitors that they should expect something above and beyond the norm—not a good thing in Lisa's estimation.

Lisa even felt a bit insulted in that Elizabeth obviously approved the "comfort" campaign, yet, since the Chief Executive Officer's arrival, she had rejected every single request of hers for improving patient and visitor comfort at Emerald Hills. Elizabeth, for example, opted against higher quality patient beds, more comfortable waiting room chairs, and so on, settling for baseline products that provided baseline comfort and nothing more.

When Lisa arrived at the medical center, she met with Elizabeth and expressed her concerns. She even went as far as citing recent patient satisfaction survey results that demonstrated that patients view Emerald Hills' comfort to be of average quality. Elizabeth confessed that Emerald Hills could indeed be more comfortable and that it was not really offering anything in the area substantively better than its competitors, but she viewed the slogan to simply be marketing puffery that patients and visitors overlook anyway.

Lisa respectfully disagreed with Elizabeth and went on to say that Emerald Hills has an ethical obligation to accurately portray itself in its advertisements. Further, by touting excellent patient care, quick service, or friendly staff members—points ranked very highly by patients in recent satisfaction surveys conducted by Emerald Hills—she noted that the medical center would be playing up its strengths, rather than overselling its average-rated comfort. Lisa also noted that it was vital for the medical center to market what it currently is, not what it wishes to be or what it might be in the future. She viewed ignorance of this to be a formula for disaster, as patient experiences will not meet and certainly will not exceed their expectations.

Lisa concluded her meeting with Elizabeth by expressing that under Donald's watch or the watch of any other informed, onsite marketing executive, the "comfort" campaign would have never occurred, especially given the many obvious strengths of Emerald Hills Medical Center in other areas. She viewed Concord Marketing to be uninformed and out of touch; ever-present risks whenever operations are outsourced. Lisa suggested to Elizabeth that she reconsider her decision to forgo hiring a capable marketing executive. Elizabeth agreed to give Lisa's suggestion some thought.

DISCUSSION

1. Lisa indicated that she was very concerned with Emerald Hills Medical Center's "comfort" campaign, viewing it to oversell the establishment. Assuming that Lisa was correct in her assessment, what likely would be the forthcoming ramifications of the campaign?

2. Elizabeth unilaterally approved the comfort-centered campaign on behalf of Emerald Hills Medical Center, yet she rejected all of Lisa's prior efforts to elevate Emerald Hills' comfort features to a point that would have validated the advertising campaign's claim. Further, Elizabeth viewed advertisements to simply represent puffery and did not believe that accountability was necessary. What does this say about Elizabeth as a Chief Executive Officer? What are your thoughts regarding Lisa's perspectives on truth and accuracy in advertising?

3. Assume that the governing board of Emerald Hills Medical Center removes Elizabeth as Chief Executive Officer and places you in that particular role. Based on the information provided in the case, what actions would you take in the area of marketing and why would you proceed in that fashion?

4. Assume that Lisa was accurate in her prediction and that the advertising campaign indeed did oversell Emerald Hills Medical Center, disappointing patients and prompting associated complaints. What steps would you suggest that the medical center take in order to recover the confidence of its patient base?

5. What are your thoughts on the viability of outsourcing top marketing leadership positions in healthcare institutions? What are the advantages and disadvantages of such? How might Elizabeth's outsourcing decision at Emerald Hills Medical Center have been improved?

CHAPTER 5

The Gamble

SNAPSHOT

Institutions:

Generations Pharma, a pharmaceutical company specializing in dietary supplements that are distributed via retail channels

Santos Research, a market research firm working on behalf of Generations Pharma

Location:

Charleston (population 114,916), located in the Pacific region of the United States

Characters:

Ms. Stephanie Grant, Chief Marketing Officer

Mr. Bill Mitchell, Chief Executive Officer

Mr. Douglas Sawyer, Founder (deceased)

(all of Generations Pharma)

Context:

In this case, the top marketing executive of a pharmaceutical company endeavors to revitalize product packaging and is met with impressive results.

Stephanie Grant, Chief Marketing Officer for Generations Pharma, has just formulated a plan to take her company's product offerings to an entirely new level. Specifically, she plans to significantly upgrade product packaging to make it more contemporary, which she believes will attract greater attention and help to reposition the offerings, making them champions instead of contenders in a field of very powerful competitors and fiercely brand-loyal customers. The stakes are high, as this represents a significant gamble, but Stephanie is confident that her efforts will result in greater fortunes, both for herself and her company.

Based in Charleston (population 114,916), located in the Pacific region of the United States, Generations Pharma specializes in the production and distribution of dietary supplements through retailers across the United States. The firm's key product offering is known as Generations Daily, a multivitamin that is taken once per day to supplement dietary intake as part of a regimen to ensure proper health and nutrition. Generations Daily accounts for 37% of the annual sales volume of Generations Pharma, making it the key product in a portfolio of 27 offerings, with most products being niche dietary supplements holding much less significance in relative terms.

Generations Daily, in fact, was the first product to be marketed by Generations Pharma, which was founded 75 years ago by Douglas Sawyer, a chemist with a penchant for developing products that addressed health and wellness. Douglas formulated a health supplement that contained a robust array of vitamins, minerals, and other nutrients to ensure good health. With excellent results from product testing, he decided to market the product under the Generations brand name because he viewed the supplement to be conducive to long-term health and believed that the brand name conjured images of longevity.

To house the multivitamins, Douglas selected unique gold packaging that prominently featured the silhouette of a butterfly, accompanied by stylized lettering permitting easy product identification. While the ingredients of Generations Daily had changed over the years, improved based on the latest scientific research on health and wellness, the packaging components of the product have endured, being lightly refreshed periodically to stay current. Packaging elements, in fact, are shared across the entire product line of Generations Pharma with only modest variations being incorporated to distinguish one item from the other. Needless to say, the gold packaging and butterfly image are firmly associated with Generations Pharma products in the minds of people familiar with dietary supplements.

The mere fact that Generations Pharma had survived 75 years served as a testament to the company's ability to adapt to the changing environment, outlasting a revolving door of competitors who entered the market over past years and decades, most ultimately failing. The firm has been and continues to be successful, but it has only rarely been able to secure premier positions in the marketplace, almost always finding its various products falling into fourth-, fifth-, and sixth-place positions in the battle for market share. Generations Daily, in a few markets, does occupy the position of market leader, but this is atypical; the product usually occupies the lower rungs of the market leadership ladder. This is sufficient for a viable business, but Stephanie wants more than simple viability.

As a growth-oriented marketer, Stephanie has long since viewed market stagnation to be a source of frustration over the course of her 7-year tenure at Generations Pharma. She is not experiencing any pressure to improve sales, as the company's Chief Executive Officer, Bill Mitchell, finds the current results to be in line with business projections. Instead, Stephanie's push for increased growth is motivated internally by her simple desire to always move one step ahead.

In investigating what possibly could be done to bolster sales, Stephanie viewed additional marketing communications to be an inappropriate pathway. As Generations Pharma products are distributed exclusively through retail channels, such as discount stores and groceries, Stephanie has worked tirelessly with these establishments to promote the company's various health and wellness offerings. She has been especially aggressive on price, frequently running special discounts advertised through the sale papers of the various retailers. While this has served to maintain market share and, at least in some cases, stimulate modest growth, the results are not as pleasing as she desires. She views additional marketing communications dollars dedicated to the product line to be wasteful as the products already are well-known and are prominently featured in advertisements and other promotional vehicles. The saturation point has been reached in Stephanie's estimation.

Probing deeper, Stephanie came to believe that, in current form, Generations Pharma products might potentially have peaked and are incapable of achieving growth without product enhancements that will attract an increasing number of buyers. Stephanie decided to comprehensively review the company's entire product portfolio from the ground up, looking for weaknesses that might be stemming growth. This required gaining the perspectives of consumers and, as Generations Pharma products are sold nationally, it was necessary for Stephanie to outsource major parts of this significant undertaking.

With Bill's endorsement, Stephanie authorized Santos Research, a market research firm specializing in buyer behavior in the retail sector, to conduct a series of focus groups across the nation with the primary goal being to ascertain consumer perspectives on dietary supplements, generally, and Generations Pharma offerings, specifically. Over a period of several months, Santos Research carried out the focus groups, with chief findings generally indicating favorable perceptions regarding Generations Pharma products and their associated performance as dietary supplements, but unfavorable perceptions regarding product packaging. Additional research conducted by Santos Research validated the findings of the focus groups.

Hearing of the negative consumer perspectives regarding the packaging of Generations Pharma products came as no surprise to Stephanie as she herself never viewed the packaging to be especially attractive. She, however, had never addressed the issue before because the company's packaging had extensive historical meaning, dating back to the origins of the company. But now that she had evidence that consumers disliked Generations Pharma's packaging, Stephanie believed that it was time to act. Having extensive work experience, along with a Master of Business Administration, she certainly knew that poor packaging could sabotage the success of otherwise excellent products. Perhaps this was the culprit that was prohibiting Generations Pharma from achieving greater success in the marketplace.

Meeting with Bill, Stephanie presented Santos Research's findings and additional data that she had collected in-house. Over multiple discussions, the two agreed that perhaps it was time to alter the company's packaging. Over subsequent weeks and months, packaging prototypes were developed and tested. Ultimately, a final version was selected. The new packaging incorporated a rainbow of colors, rather than the gold containers of the past. Gone, too, was the butterfly, being replaced by a multicolor depiction of people, designed to resemble a family, holding hands to form a ring. These revolutionary changes completely altered the look and feel of Generations Pharma products. Focus groups loved the comprehensive revision, indicating the potential for increased visibility and sales of Generations Pharma products in the market.

The national rollout of Generations Pharma products in their new packaging ensued shortly thereafter, complemented by a robust television and magazine advertising campaign heralding the upgrade, noting that the same great Generations Pharma products now had new, exciting packaging to better represent the enclosed health and wellness contents. One month after the rollout, sales reached an all-time high for the given period, with product orders from retailers being received at a record pace. Stephanie was ecstatic.

DISCUSSION

1. In this case, Stephanie gambles that enhanced packaging will improve the sales of Generations Pharma products and it appears that her gamble has paid off. The gamble was perhaps all the more risky in that the company's sales were deemed by Bill to be meeting expectations. While enhanced packaging might be viewed to facilitate sales, it also could result in adverse consequences, especially given the lengthy history of the company's packaging. Discuss the upside potential and downside risks associated with altering packaging, especially for products that are already experiencing satisfactory sales. How would you go about determining if the potential benefits outweigh the associated risks involved with such alterations?

2. What are your thoughts on the manner in which Stephanie went about investigating consumer perspectives of the product offerings provided by Generations Pharma? Prepare a critical review of the process initiated by Stephanie. Would you make any changes? Why or why not?

3. Prior to engaging in comprehensive investigations of the product offerings of Generations Pharma, Stephanie opted against directing more resources to marketing communications, indicating that she believed that the saturation point had been reached. This showed discipline as some individuals are of the belief that throwing additional money into advertising and other forms of marketing communication serves as the catch-all answer to marketing problems. How would you go about determining cut-off points after which additional marketing communications funds will not be extended?

4. Stephanie's gamble could just have easily had the reverse effect, resulting in declining sales. While it might seem that upgraded packaging would naturally yield better sales results, there are no guarantees. What might prompt declining sales in the face of major packaging upgrades?

5. This case dealt with healthcare goods, as opposed to services. Just as goods can be packaged, so too can services. Provide a detailed overview of the elements that constitute the packaging of services in the healthcare industry.

6

The Name Game

SNAPSHOT

Institutions:
Ridgecrest Medical Center, a 315-bed, for-profit healthcare institution providing general medical and surgical services
Robinson-Martinez Hospital, a 275-bed, for-profit medical establishment providing general medical and surgical services

Location:
Union (population 411,015), located in the Middle Atlantic region of the United States

Character:
Mr. Brian Garcia, Chief Executive Officer, Ridgecrest Medical Center

Context:
In this case, the top executive of a medical center reflects on a number of branding considerations emerging as a result of his institution's recent acquisition of a competing hospital.

Brian Garcia, Chief Executive Officer of Ridgecrest Medical Center, has a dilemma, but unlike many dilemmas, this one fortunately is the result of a pleasing development and he is eager to craft a resolution. After intensive and lengthy negotiations, Ridgecrest Medical Center has agreed to purchase another comprehensive health service provider in the community, Robinson-Martinez Hospital. While many details of this recent development remain to be addressed, Brian has decided to dedicate a few hours during his afternoon to work through a few branding issues concerning the acquisition, with his major task being to formulate an identity management plan that will yield optimal results.

While acquisition activities inevitably foster branding dilemmas, the particular branding situation emanating from Ridgecrest's acquisition of Robinson-Martinez Hospital is especially complex as, in Brian's view, there is not an obvious branding direction to pursue. Strengths and weaknesses are possessed by both entities, with neither possessing significant benefits over one another.

Ridgecrest Medical Center and Robinson-Martinez Hospital, named for two local pioneers in health services, both are located in Union, a city of 411,015 located in the Middle Atlantic region of the United States. The two facilities exist in a very competitive marketplace that includes a total of seven comprehensive health service providers. Ridgecrest and Robinson-Martinez are, in fact, very similar facilities. They both are for-profit, offer similar service arrays, and serve similar target markets. Bed sizes differ slightly, with Ridgecrest having slightly more at 315, compared to Robinson-Martinez at 275.

Both Ridgecrest and Robinson-Martinez hold the fourth and fifth market share positions in the community, but when merged, the unified facility will move up to third place. This is a highly desirable position, as it will place the new establishment in one of the top three slots in the community, giving it associated bragging rights and positioning the institution within striking distance of first place.

Geographically, Ridgecrest is located on the north side of Union, while Robinson-Martinez is located on the south side of the city. This is viewed very positively in that it will extend the reach of Ridgecrest into areas of the city that previously were difficult to penetrate as a result of distance. Brian also is pleased that studies leading up to the purchase of Robinson-Martinez Hospital indicated that the two facilities possessed highly compatible cultures, increasing the likelihood of success as a single institution. Fortunately, the acquisition represents a perfect match, pleasing everyone involved—stockholders, governing board members, executive teams, clinicians, and all other employees.

As Ridgecrest is the purchaser, branding decisions rest with its governing board; however, this group traditionally has looked to Brian for advice on complex decisions and the branding issue likely will be no exception. Using his typical approach, Brian will formulate a series of options for the Ridgecrest board, craft strengths and weaknesses associated with each, and will forward a recommendation based on his analysis. Only rarely has the board gone against Brian's recommendation, so the likelihood of acceptance of his recommendation is high, compelling him to work feverishly to craft a brand name that will ensure the best possible marketplace results.

Brian is no stranger to branding as he initially served in various healthcare marketing positions over a 20-year period before being elevated to the top leadership position at Ridgecrest 7 years ago, his first position at the helm of a healthcare entity. He well knows that much is at stake with the current branding decision at hand as missteps could send the wrong message to customers.

Even with the emergence of a well-conceived brand name, Brian realizes that altering identities that have long been recognized, accepted, and appreciated by patients has the potential to create massive confusion that might harm Ridgecrest. He views the confusion to be especially associated with the brand name alterations of medical care facilities as such changes naturally beget patient inquiries and concerns such as whether their providers will remain on staff, whether their health insurance will continue to be accepted by newly branded institutions, and so on. As Brian begins his afternoon brainstorming session, he carefully reminds himself of the public relations issues that must be addressed whenever identities are altered. Such public relations activities, of course, come after the branding decision is made, but Brian knows that it is best to continually think about future steps and associated outcomes whenever identity management decisions are at hand.

In his afternoon brainstorming session, Brian begins his investigation by reviewing the elements of identity used by both Ridgecrest and Robinson-Martinez. He also reviews a number of marketing research documents pertaining to consumer perceptions of the two brands at hand and associated variables, such as quality, convenience, and so on.

With a good understanding of each organization's identity and associated consumer perspectives, Brian then proceeds to reflect first on the matter of determining the brand name for the unified institution, saving other brand manifestations such as color, symbolism, and so on, for later consideration. Working his way through the possibilities, Brian sought to narrow down the options. Should the two entities be permitted to retain their respective identities (i.e., Ridgecrest Medical Center and Robinson-Martinez Hospital)? If so, should an umbrella brand be created and added to each institution's brand name as a means of showing interconnections between facilities (e.g., CarePlus–Ridgecrest Medical Center, CarePlus–Robinson-Martinez Hospital)? Perhaps the two brand names could be combined, permitting both to remain, at least in some sort of merged capacity (e.g., Ridgecrest–Robinson-Martinez Medical Center, RRM Medical Center)? Maybe Ridgecrest should be rebranded Ridgecrest-North, with Robinson-Martinez being renamed Ridgecrest-South? Maybe Robinson-Martinez should be renamed Robinson-Martinez–South, with Ridgecrest being renamed Robinson-Martinez–North? Maybe both Ridgecrest and Robinson-Martinez identities should be scrapped, opting instead for a new brand name for the resulting institution? Each question begets other questions.

Recent marketing research indicates that both Ridgecrest and Robinson-Martinez possess high brand recognition in the community, with Ridgecrest having a slight edge over Robinson-Martinez. This fact eliminates the easy decision of simply taking the stronger brand identity and applying it to the facility with the weaker brand identity. Ridgecrest is the newer facility, being established just 20 years ago, making it several times younger than Robinson-Martinez, which possesses a 100-year history in Union. How should these very different histories weigh on the branding decision? How should the tribute to Robinson and Martinez, two prominent individuals who were credited with elevating the quality of health services in Union over a century ago, be handled in the branding decision? Both facilities have very loyal followings and are held in high regard by their respective clientele. Would the elimination of one or both brands create confusion or possibly ill will on the part of respective customer bases?

After about 2 hours of debate, Brian had not made much progress toward resolution, but he had taken the pivotal step of initiating the process and had begun to craft a framework for formulating branding options. As the branding process draws on creativity, he knows that with continual thought and attention over the coming days, ideas will begin to pop into his head. Then, following a few focus groups to test brand names and ideas, as well as detailed discussions with his senior management team, he anticipates that he will be in the position to formulate an associated report for Ridgecrest Medical Center's governing board.

DISCUSSION

1. Brian faces a very tough branding decision resulting from Ridgecrest Medical Center's acquisition of Robinson-Martinez Hospital. Assume that you are in Brian's position and that you have learned that the governing board desires to adopt a single brand name for both institutions. What would you choose and why?

2. Once the task of formulating a brand name has been effected, other branding elements must be addressed, including color schemes, fonts, symbols, and so on, which come together to form a logo. Based on your own preferences regarding color and design, take the brand name you selected in Inquiry 1 and develop a logo for the new institution. While a hand-drawn sketch will suffice, a design using graphics software is preferred. Supply a brief narrative describing your logo and be sure to include your rationale for selecting associated style elements.

3. Assume that the governing board accepts your branding recommendation as presented in the earlier inquiries. What are your next steps from a marketing perspective? In your discussion, be sure to address the public relations aspect, among other marketing matters that will need attention.

4. Brian noted the potentially sensitive issue of removing the Robinson and Martinez names from the new brand identity. How should named institutions be handled in such cases? What obligations, if any, do institutions have in retaining the names of those memorialized or commemorated in brands? Please justify your perspectives.

5. Assume that the roles are reversed, with Robinson-Martinez Hospital acquiring Ridgecrest Medical Center. Would this change your brand name selection as devised when Ridgecrest was the overtaking party? Why or why not?

CHAPTER 7

The Weakest Link

SNAPSHOT

Institutions:

Montrose Urgent Care Center, a clinic, owned and operated by Montrose Health System, that specializes in urgent care medical services

Montrose Health System, a not-for-profit health system consisting of four medical centers and numerous ancillary components

Location:

Waverly (population 365,272), located in the West North Central region of the United States

Characters:

Mr. Andrew Billingsley, Administrator
Ms. Victoria Forsythe, Assistant Administrator
Ms. Judy Henderson, Part-time Admissions Clerk
(all of Montrose Urgent Care Center)
Ms. Patricia Kelly, Vice President of Marketing, Montrose Health System

Context:

In this case, the administrator of an urgent care center investigates an unusual pattern observed in patient satisfaction survey results.

Andrew Billingsley, Administrator of Montrose Urgent Care Center, is confused. Patient satisfaction survey results are inconsistent across the month, with high levels of satisfaction dominating the time frame, punctuated by very brief periods of lower patient satisfaction, making for an interesting trend line. Andrew is committed to achieving a consistently high level of satisfaction and, therefore, intends to identify the culprit that is causing the unusual, brief decline in satisfaction that periodically appears over the course of each given month. While he is pleased that aggregate results are indicating very positive experiences and that high levels of patient satisfaction generally rule, the anomaly of the negative instance witnessed from time to time is proving to be annoying. He sets his sights on resolving this matter.

Montrose Urgent Care Center is located in Waverly, a city of 365,272 located in the West North Central region of the United States. As indicated by its name, the center specializes in urgent care medicine and is owned and operated by Montrose Health System, a multihospital not-for-profit provider of healthcare services. Montrose Urgent Care Center fills a critical role in the community for the delivery of medical services that require immediate attention but are not acute enough to warrant treatment in a hospital's emergency department. This ultimately helps to contain healthcare costs by addressing injuries and illnesses that otherwise would be directed to the much more expensive emergency medicine setting. Montrose Urgent Care Center holds extensive hours of operation—7 AM to 8 PM, 7 days per week—making the clinic one of the most accessible healthcare establishments in Waverly from the perspective of hours of availability.

A healthcare industry veteran of 20 years, serving primarily in nursing positions before moving into the area of management, Andrew has served as Administrator of Montrose Urgent Care Center for only 6 months and he gradually has been acclimating himself to operations in this new environment. Having gained familiarity with core operations, he decided to focus his sights on better understanding ancillary areas that are vital to the establishment's performance. One such area is patient satisfaction.

As part of its commitment to quality, Montrose Health System effects a comprehensive patient satisfaction survey, with instruments being tailored for each of its many units, permitting specific, unit-applicable inquiries to be forwarded to patients. The surveys are conducted via touch-screen computer, with patients being asked at discharge to complete the brief instrument that gives them the opportunity to comment on their patient experience. On completion, the surveys are electronically forwarded to a database that is accessible by analysts in Montrose Health System's Department of Marketing. On a monthly basis, analysts process the data and forward reports of patient satisfaction survey results to given units, permitting employees to have a better understanding of their efforts to meet patient wants and needs.

Patient satisfaction is important not only for best attending to the wants and needs of patients, but also for the urgent care center and its employees, as performance is taken into consideration in system resource allocations. Andrew set aside some time to get a better understanding of the patient satisfaction results garnered by Montrose Urgent Care Center. As Montrose Health System has been engaging in patient satisfaction using the current survey instrument and method of administration for 10 months, Andrew had access to 10 monthly reports for the urgent care center. This was not the best of situations, as he would have liked the opportunity to study a couple of years of data, but not the worst of situations, as he might not have had access to any historical data at all.

In his initial review, Andrew was pleasantly surprised by the aggregate monthly performance indicators, showing high levels of patient satisfaction across the core measurement areas of facilities, admissions, physicians, nurses, and ancillary personnel. Further, patients indicated that they would be highly likely to visit Montrose Urgent Care Center for future medical wants and needs and also indicated that they would be highly likely to refer others to the establishment for care and attention. To Andrew, this was exactly what he had hoped to witness.

On closer examination, however, Andrew noticed an interesting pattern. Specifically, he observed that on many of the weeks within given months, a marked downward trend in satisfaction occurred on Fridays. The patient satisfaction levels recorded on those particular days were very low, representing an average reduction of 50% from the results typically achieved on all other days of the week. While the deviation was rare and did not have a tremendously negative impact on aggregate results, given that it represented only one day per week, Andrew believed that it was essential to probe into the matter, as whatever was negatively impacting patient satisfaction results on that given day could become epidemic, creating a greater tow on aggregate results. Further, Andrew was a perfectionist and believed that any instance of reduced service, as perceived by customers, was worthy of investigation and rectification.

In seeking to get to the bottom of the matter, Andrew acquired the staffing schedules over the past few months to see if he could detect a staffing pattern associated with the sharp, but very brief, Friday decline, but he could not detect anything initially. On further investigation, however, he discovered that, on Fridays only, a part-time Admissions Clerk, Judy Henderson, regularly worked during the afternoons and evenings. Andrew knew that he could isolate the problem if he could obtain data over the course of given dayparts, since Judy only worked during a defined time period on Fridays. He contacted Montrose Health System's Vice President of Marketing, Patricia Kelly, who coordinated patient satisfaction efforts system-wide, to investigate the possibility of securing more specific data.

Patricia was appreciative that one of the system's managers took the initiative to probe deeper into given patient satisfaction results. As the surveys were conducted via touch-screen computer, instruments were not only date stamped, but also time stamped, permitting given units the opportunity to examine patient satisfaction survey results as they occur over the course of daily operations. Patricia supplied detailed reports that permitted Andrew to isolate the poor patient satisfaction results to the afternoons and evenings of each Friday. As the personnel mix, with the exception of Judy, occurred on other days of the week, which did not involve declining patient satisfaction, it became obvious that Judy likely was the source of the problem.

With newfound enlightenment on the issue, Andrew met with Victoria Forsythe, the clinic's Assistant Administrator, to discuss his findings and seek additional insights. Victoria had been employed at Montrose Urgent Care Center for 2 years, something Andrew hoped would give her insights that could shed light on Judy's performance and other possible culprits.

On sharing his information, Victoria replied that she was not very surprised to learn that Judy was undermining patient satisfaction performance. She, like other part-time personnel, was used for the purpose of covering scheduling gaps, which arose due to the center's expansive hours of operation. Judy had served for 17 years as an admissions clerk at Montrose Urgent Care Center, but retired 3 years ago. The clinic turned to her for the provision of periodic coverage. For well over 1 year,

Judy has been working the afternoon and evening schedule on Fridays. Victoria indicated that Judy was very familiar with the operations of the center and was very reliable, but that she lacked the personality to deal effectively with the public, often coming across as being rather blunt. The issue was not severe enough to warrant disciplinary action, but, according to Victoria, her curt mannerisms were very noticeable to other staff members and patients.

After further discussions regarding Judy and her history of performance, Andrew and Victoria took the time to examine the more specific data that he had obtained from Patricia. Andrew found it particularly interesting that the negative perspectives of patients occurring over the Friday afternoon and evening periods were harshest regarding aspects of admissions, but bled over to other areas of inquiry, such as those regarding physicians and nurses, negatively impacting them as well. From Andrew's perspective, this provided further justification for addressing and remedying the given weakness, as one curt employee along a chain of pleasant employees clearly has the potential to damage an otherwise excellent patient experience. He and Victoria discuss their options.

DISCUSSION

1. In this case, Andrew investigates an anomaly witnessed in patient satisfaction survey results and appears to have isolated the cause to a single person, Judy. Assuming that Judy was found to indeed be the culprit, what actions would you take to rectify the matter and why?

2. This case illustrates that despite the successful delivery of a core product, in this case, patient care services, ancillary personnel who are not customer oriented have the potential to cast a negative light on an otherwise excellent patient experience. What does this case say about the necessity of ensuring that every single employee in healthcare institutions serves as a customer service ambassador?

3. Montrose Health System effects patient satisfaction surveys in an interesting manner by using touch-screen computers, as opposed to other forms of administration. Investigate common techniques used for administering surveys and provide an assessment of their strengths and weaknesses. Which method do you prefer and why?

4. Although aggregate survey results were highly acceptable, Andrew probed deeper into the patient satisfaction results of Montrose Urgent Care Center in an effort to resolve the periodic but very brief satisfaction declines witnessed over time. Andrew indicated that he was interested in resolving the results anomaly because its source could become epidemic and further diminish aggregate results. What benefits does the proactive attitude held by Andrew provide to healthcare organizations and the employees holding such attitudes? If you were in Andrew's position, would you have been so proactive?

5. Andrew was willing not only to examine the findings of patient satisfaction surveys, but also to act on the results. What are your thoughts on the use of patient satisfaction survey findings in healthcare organizations? Do you think that healthcare entities fail to make the best use of the information provided by these instruments? Why or why not?

PART TWO

Marketing Communications

CHAPTER 8

Missed Opportunities

SNAPSHOT

Institutions:
Briarwood Medical Center, a 550-bed, not-for-profit institution offering general medical and surgical services
Crestview Hospital, a 475-bed, for-profit establishment providing general medical and surgical services

Location:
Oakland (population 204,086), located in the East South Central region of the United States

Characters:
Mr. Michael Anderson, Chief Executive Officer
Ms. Susan Daniels, Chief Marketing Officer
Ms. Pamela Goldman, Board President
Mr. Frank Miller, Chief Executive Officer (retired)
(all of Briarwood Medical Center)
Mr. Steve Williams, Sales Representative, Southeastern Outdoor

Context:
In this case, the top marketing officer of a medical center attempts to secure two billboards occupying a prized location, but her request is rejected by the institution's chief executive officer, leading to a rather precarious situation.

Susan Daniels, Chief Marketing Officer at Briarwood Medical Center, has been on a roller coaster ride that unfortunately ended on a low point. This all started 1 month ago when she received a telephone call from Steve Williams, a sales representative from Southeastern Outdoor. Much to Susan's surprise, Steve communicated that both facings of a billboard located adjacent to Briarwood Medical Center would be available at the end of the month. The two panels had long been leased by State Street Paints, a family-owned company that recently communicated that it was going out of business after 35 years of service. For the first time in years, the panels were available, presenting an excellent marketing communications opportunity for Briarwood Medical Center because the billboard panels, situated on the main traffic corridor running by the establishment, were located in such proximity that they appeared to be placed on medical center property.

Steve knew that Susan had been very interested in securing the panels for Briarwood Medical Center and he also knew that the ideal location of the panels made the establishment an obvious lessee. On learning of the availabilities, Susan found it difficult to contain her enthusiasm. She was very much aware that the panels offered countless opportunities to market the medical center and believed that they would be excellent investments. This was especially the case as Briarwood Medical Center was entangled in a seemingly endless battle for market share against a skilled competitor, making every opportunity to win patients crucial.

Briarwood Medical Center, a 550-bed, not-for-profit healthcare establishment, is based in Oakland, a city of 204,086 residents located in the East South Central region of the United States. It competes against an aggressive for-profit competitor, Crestview Hospital, a 475-bed facility providing roughly parallel services in the same market. Briarwood is the more historic of the two institutions, having been founded 75 years ago, and traditionally enjoyed decades of market leadership as a result of being the best practices provider in Oakland, outpacing competitors on every level. However, Briarwood Medical Center's market position began to change 20 years ago with the introduction of Crestview Hospital into the market. For the first time in its history, Briarwood Medical Center faced a competitor that challenged each and every competitive advantage possessed by the institution, a feat made even more difficult given Crestview Hospital's close proximity, located just 2 miles away from Briarwood on the same roadway, State Street.

Briarwood Medical Center initially struggled in this new environment, slowly losing market share for a decade. Poor results led Briarwood's governing board to appoint a new management team, of which Susan was a member, and the fortunes of the institution began to change thereafter. Briarwood eventually recaptured much of its lost market share, giving it a small edge over Crestview Hospital in the market leadership battle. Much of Briarwood Medical Center's success has been credited to Susan as she was the architect of the establishment's marketing initiatives, which helped restore competitiveness and prosperity.

An aggressive marketer, Susan intended to acquire the soon-to-be-available billboard panels, but one problem stood in her way—Briarwood's new Chief Executive Officer, Michael Anderson. Michael was hired 6 months ago, replacing the retiring Frank Miller, a member of Briarwood's turnaround team who was appointed along with Susan 10 years ago. In recent meetings, Susan has come to realize that Michael does not respect the discipline of marketing, especially its advertising component, viewing patient traffic simply to be the result of physician referrals or insurance coverage mandates.

Susan knew better and she had data to support her position. While physician referrals and insurance coverage do influence patient traffic, so do marketing communications, among many other things. Her research indicated that many patients have the opportunity to select most any healthcare provider in Oakland, as most insurance plans offered in the community permit at least some degree of choice. And most physicians in the area have privileges at multiple hospitals in the community. Given this, patients have a choice as to where they receive medical services, something that, at least in part, is influenced by marketing communications.

In fact, Susan's recent patient satisfaction survey indicated that 42% of new patients were at least somewhat influenced to visit Briarwood Medical Center as a result of its advertisements. She, too, was very aware of those patients who do not have a relationship with any medical provider, knowing that these patients often look to advertising, among other things, as they go about making their patronage decisions. And this did not even begin to address the value of marketing communications in influencing patronage in the area of elective services. Despite Susan's evidence and rationale, Michael remained unconvinced, viewing advertising to be a cost rather than an investment.

Given this history, Susan knew that convincing Michael to support the purchase of the billboards would be very difficult but, undeterred, she scheduled a meeting with him to discuss the billboard lease. Because her advertising budget was already committed to other initiatives, she did not have the funds necessary to secure the panels and therefore needed access to additional resources. Each of the two panels costs $2500 per month for a total lease fee of $30,000 over the 6-month contract period—the minimum term available. In the meeting, Susan made a compelling case for leasing the billboard panels, but Michael emphatically rejected her request and noted that he believed Briarwood was already spending too much money on advertising.

After the meeting, Susan began to ponder the fate of Briarwood Medical Center under a leader who ignored factual information and failed to acknowledge that marketing efforts largely were responsible for Briarwood's turnaround 10 years ago. Susan knew that many board members were heavily supportive of marketing initiatives, having witnessed associated results over the years, but she felt as though she could not break the chain of command to ask for their assistance. Given Michael's resistance, Susan believed that she had no other choice than to forfeit the billboard opportunity.

A few weeks pass and, with a new month beginning, Susan set out to work on a bright Monday morning. As she drove down State Street, about to turn into Briarwood's employee parking lot, her eyes glanced up at the north facing of the billboard she had been so desirous of securing. Her heart nearly stopped. Listed in bold letters and bright colors right before her eyes was the billboard of Crestview Hospital. Briarwood's arch rival had secured not just one facing, but both facings, situated in perfect view of patients entering and leaving Briarwood Medical Center from either direction on the heavily traveled State Street. And the tag line used in the ads—*The Best Medical Care in Oakland*—did not help matters. Given the proximity of the panels to campus, it was almost like Briarwood Medical Center was promoting Crestview Hospital. Susan was crushed.

Immediately on making her way into her office, Susan received a telephone call from Pamela Goldman, President of Briarwood's governing board, and she was furious. Pamela had tried to reach Michael for an explanation as to how Briarwood allowed this to happen, but he had not responded, so she decided to contact Susan for answers. Susan, equally outraged, was more than happy to enlighten Pamela on the past few weeks at Briarwood Medical Center.

DISCUSSION

1. Susan found Crestview Hospital's new billboard postings to be especially troubling because they were placed in a location directly adjacent to Briarwood Medical Center. What do you see as the possible ramifications of these postings for Briarwood Medical Center? For example, how might patients of the establishment react? What about other community stakeholders?

2. Michael thwarted an opportunity to secure the prized billboards, seemingly resulting from negative views of marketing generally and advertising specifically. Despite solid evidence of the benefits of marketing and advertising when used appropriately, some in the healthcare industry possess views similar to those held by Michael. Why do you think this is the case?

3. What actions do you believe Briarwood Medical Center should take to counter Crestview Hospital's new billboard postings? Assuming that the governing board mandates that additional advertising funds be forwarded to Susan for bolstering Briarwood's advertising initiatives, how would you recommend that these funds be spent? Please justify your recommendations.

4. Pamela seemed very upset about Crestview Hospital's billboards and she demanded answers. As the case concluded, it appeared that Susan was about to provide those answers, likely pointing the finger at Michael. Given the billboard debacle, how should Briarwood Medical Center's governing board address Michael? Do you see his tenure at Briarwood threatened? Why or why not?

5. Susan appeared to struggle with whether she should contact Briarwood Medical Center's governing board when Michael rejected her request. She knew the board members very well, given her years of service at Briarwood, but she opted to respect the chain of command. Had you been in Susan's position, what action would you have taken and why?

Unanticipated Consequences

Matthew Fields, Vice President of Marketing at White Rose Medical Center, is cautiously optimistic. He has just committed resources to an advertising method never before used by his establishment and he has high hopes that his gamble will yield excellent results. Specifically, Matthew has decided to promote White Rose Medical Center using cinema advertising and he has just signed a contract for such with Vista Cinemas, the largest theater chain in the region, providing one 30-second spot featuring White Rose Medical Center to theater audiences prior to each movie shown over the course of a 3-month contract period.

White Rose Medical Center is a financially sound, well-operated general health and medical facility located in Newcastle, a city of 113,544 situated in the West North Central region of the United States. The not-for-profit, 325-bed establishment competes with four comprehensive healthcare providers in the city. As might be expected, these systems compete vigorously with one another in the battle for market share, something that compels Matthew to be especially innovative in his efforts to reach and attract target audiences in Newcastle and the surrounding region.

Outshopping is not much of an issue for the healthcare providers in Newcastle, the physical center and largest city of an expansive geographic region. As most of the surrounding area is rural, consisting of several moderately sized cities and many small communities, residents across the region look to Newcastle's comprehensive medical care providers to deliver the vast majority of their healthcare wants and needs. Given the market captivity, the greatest threat faced by White Rose Medical Center is not from out-of-market competitors, but from Newcastle's other medical providers.

Formally trained in marketing at both the undergraduate and graduate levels, Matthew has led the marketing operations of White Rose Medical Center for 12 years and he is largely credited with achieving and maintaining the medical center's razor thin market leadership position over its arch rival, the for-profit Century Medical Center. With such a small margin separating the two facilities, Matthew understands the importance of consistently communicating White Rose Medical Center's benefits to target populations in the region and he does this very well.

In accordance with guidance from his marketing education, Matthew's approach to marketing communications is consistent with textbook recommendations. He meticulously formulates the marketing communications mix, investigating advertising, public relations, personal selling, sales promotion, and direct marketing opportunities in the context of given promotions goals and objectives, selecting the mix that he believes will best accomplish designated mandates. Importantly, Matthew does not simply throw caution to the wind and hope that marketing communications deliver results; instead, he studies various communicative mechanisms and establishes methods for measuring results.

He operates on a strict mandate that if he cannot measure the results of a given marketing communications device, he does not make the purchase. Just as with any progressive marketer, Matthew always keeps an eye out for new opportunities to communicate with target audiences. In fact, this mindset is exactly what led to his decision to try cinema advertising, prompted by a recent visit from Veronica Mitchell, a sales representative for Vista Cinemas.

Vista Cinemas is the region's largest movie theater chain, operating 12 theater complexes for a grand total of 48 screens, each typically running up to five movies per day on a 7-day per week basis. Vista has long been running coming attractions and concession promotions in the 10-minute period preceding its movies, but it only recently began to offer opportunities for businesses to purchase advertisements in the time slots situated just before feature presentations begin.

After studying data supplied by Veronica, Matthew was impressed. Vista Cinemas intentionally selected highly diverse movie mixes to attract equally broad cross-sections of the population, a "something for everyone" approach to entertainment. Matthew did not see this approach to be problematic; in fact, he viewed it to be a benefit, especially given that White Rose Medical Center provided services that were equally diverse, spanning the gamut of human life. Given this, he believed that a general advertisement reminding audiences of the excellent care and attention that one receives at White Rose Medical Center would yield optimal results.

Veronica suggested a 3-month package that provided roughly 20,000 advertising impressions—one 30-second advertisement presented prior to each of the feature presentations playing over the contract period—reaching an estimated 600,000 viewers. She emphasized that moviegoers would all largely be focused on the advertisement, given their relative captivity as they await feature presentations, making for high levels of attention.

As with any medium of advertising that he had no prior experience using, Matthew was somewhat hesitant, but he decided to proceed when Veronica offered him a very economical introductory rate over the 3-month term. He supplied the marketing communication—essentially an enhanced version of an existing 30-second television advertisement providing a general portrayal of White Rose Medical Center—and awaited the deployment of the cinema advertising campaign, which was scheduled to begin the following month.

The new month began on a Saturday, one of the biggest movie days, ushering in White Rose Medical Center's debut on the big screen. That evening, Matthew made a point to attend a movie playing at one of Vista's theaters in Newcastle to view White Rose's advertisement firsthand. The White Rose advertisement ran as promised, wedged between the coming attractions and feature presentation. Matthew was unable to ascertain much from the audience, given the low light, but the level of attentiveness certainly appeared to be very high, especially given the placement of White Rose's advertisement in such close proximity to the feature film. Leaving the theater, the potential of cinema advertising began to dawn on him.

On arriving at his office on Monday morning, he was surprised to find that the voice mailbox of White Rose Medical Center's community relations hotline, a line provided by the medical center to solicit suggestions from patients and other community stakeholders, was overflowing. No less than 50 messages were left, all of them from angry moviegoers, furious at White Rose Medical Center for running cinema advertisements.

The messages from callers were highly varied in tone and approach, but they shared a common theme. Callers viewed movies to represent a sort of escape from their daily lives and they expected that escape to be commercial free, especially given the costs of attending movies. Most callers expressed their disappointment and some current patients even communicated that they would look to other providers in the region if White Rose continued the advertisements. A few even mentioned that if the advertisements had been related to entertainment, such as those of dining establishments or recreation facilities, they would not have taken offense, but they viewed healthcare advertisements to be out of place in the movie environment. The worst messages were from a handful of callers who threatened to boycott the medical center if it did not remove the advertisements. These were all serious threats—especially given the tight battle for market leadership between White Rose and Century Medical Center—and Matthew well knew that the negative word-of-mouth would be brutal.

Needless to say, Matthew's initial feeling of confidence that cinema advertising just might be a good thing for White Rose Medical Center was quickly diffused, turning what he thought to be a boom into a bust. He contacted Veronica and asked her to pull the cinema advertisements.

DISCUSSION

1. When White Rose Medical Center's cinema advertisements were initiated, callers immediately began leaving messages of protest on the medical center's community relations hotline, generally indicating that their movie experience was violated by the advertisements. Placing yourself in the role of a moviegoer, do you view such advertisements in the same way? Why or why not? How does the particular product advertised factor into your decision?

2. On listening to the protest messages on White Rose's hotline, Matthew immediately decided to pull the cinema advertisements; this despite the advertisements having only been running for 2 days. Do you think this move was wise? Why or why not?

3. Based on protests, the White Rose cinema advertising campaign offended at least some moviegoers. Assuming that the negative sentiment was widespread and the campaign indeed missed the mark, what could Matthew have done differently to reach cinema audiences via marketing communications in a manner that would make sense and not be offensive? For this inquiry, you are encouraged to think very creatively.

4. Matthew selected a cinema advertising package that provided one 30-second spot prior to each movie, regardless of its content or rating, over the contract period. Casting aside questions of whether cinema advertising is or is not beneficial to healthcare institutions, do you think acceptance of such a package is appropriate, given that some of the movies shown over the course of the contract period might possess themes that would be unbecoming for healthcare entities? Be sure to supply the rationale behind your response.

5. What lessons does this case provide for healthcare institutions in how they go about selecting various marketing communications mechanisms upon which they engage target audiences?

CHAPTER 10

Advertising Doesn't Work

SNAPSHOT

Institution:
Brookwood Vision Center, an established provider of ophthalmology services, including laser vision correction

Location:
Stanford (population 261,370), located in the Middle Atlantic region of the United States

Characters:
Ms. Joyce Evans, Administrator
Dr. George Thomas, Owner and Ophthalmologist
(both of Brookwood Vision Center)

Context:
In this case, the administrator of an ophthalmology practice convinces its physician owner to invest in advertising but is criticized when the campaign does not deliver immediate results.

Joyce Evans, Administrator of Brookwood Vision Center, is excited about a new idea. Specifically, she believes that she has found an avenue to increase patient volume in a very cost-effective manner. A long-time nurse who worked her way into the administrative position she currently holds, Joyce has been pursuing her Master of Business Administration at a local university and is currently enrolled in a marketing course. In this course, she has been exposed to various marketing communications options and their associated costs and benefits. She has come to realize that billboard advertising has the potential to benefit Brookwood Vision Center.

Joyce has learned that billboards possess many advantages that likely will prove to be beneficial for Brookwood and, compared with other mass media, they seem to be very economical. She is especially pleased that, despite only recently beginning her graduate coursework, she already has witnessed very practical insights that have the potential to directly benefit Brookwood Vision Center, with her billboard idea being the latest. She cannot wait to communicate the information to Brookwood's owner, Dr. George Thomas.

Dr. Thomas established Brookwood Vision Center 15 years ago. Based in Stanford (population 261,370), located in the Middle Atlantic region of the United States, the practice is a full-service provider of vision services ranging from basic eye examinations to laser eye surgery services that correct vision and address other conditions of the eye. Brookwood is highly regarded for its laser vision correction services, but competition is at a fever pitch in the community, making every patient count in the battle for market share among the dozen or so providers in the immediate area.

Joyce has been associated with Brookwood Vision Center for 5 years, being recruited by Dr. Thomas from another eye surgery practice where she served as a nurse. Managing a staff of seven, she supervises all administrative operations of the establishment, ranging from human resources to medical billing, permitting Dr. Thomas to concentrate exclusively on his clinical work.

As for marketing, Joyce is in charge of that administrative aspect as well. But the more she learns in her marketing course, the more she realizes that Brookwood is failing to capitalize on opportunities that are hiding in plain sight. The clinic does engage in marketing communications activities, but only in fairly restrictive areas.

Brookwood is most reliant on provider referrals from well-cultivated relationships in the medical care marketplace. These relationships are maintained from periodic courtesy calls where Joyce visits various medical establishments in the marketplace, distributes the latest information on associated eye services, and hands out various promotional items such as key rings, pens, paperweights, and so on, all incorporating the logo and contact information of Brookwood Vision Center.

Additionally, Brookwood sponsors a variety of activities and events, ranging from sporting engagements to science festivals to band camps, for local schools and universities. This has resulted in high visibility for the clinic at events that are both educational and entertaining, attracting broad cross sections of the population and exposing them to the Brookwood brand.

Another sizeable component of Brookwood's marketing efforts pertains to public relations. The clinic occasionally holds free vision screenings at various establishments, such as grocery stores and other retail organizations. These efforts are promoted via press releases that are forwarded to area media outlets that, in turn, communicate the events to their audiences, giving Brookwood Vision Center a significant boost in visibility in the community. Free seminars on eye health also are held regularly, with press releases and word of mouth being the primary means of event communication.

Beyond that, Brookwood does very little in the way of marketing communications, with not a penny spent on advertising. This, Joyce has come to believe, is hampering what might otherwise be greater success in the marketplace.

From her marketing studies, she believes that an excellent starting point would be billboard advertising due to the excellent reach and frequency generated by the medium at a relatively low cost compared to other mass media. She also believes that this would represent a less aggressive step into advertising for Brookwood Vision Center, something she viewed to be essential given the clinic's reluctance to use advertising in the past.

Joyce did her homework. She contacted a local outdoor advertising agency and acquired cost figures for a 35 GRP (gross rating points) "showing" that promises the exposure of 35% of Stanford's population aged 18 and older to the advertisements on a daily basis. The 35 GRP constituted three bulletins, 14' × 48' panels located in different regions of the city, for a total cost of $6000 per month. A 6-month lease was required, making for a $36,000 commitment should Brookwood Vision Center decide to pursue this course of action.

Armed with facts and figures, Joyce scheduled an appointment with Dr. Thomas where the two discussed her new idea. Dr. Thomas was extremely appreciative of Joyce's efforts but he was very skeptical of advertising generally and billboard advertising specifically. He just did not view advertising to drive patronage of healthcare services, where he viewed other forms of communication, such as relationship building through personal courtesy calls, to be more effective.

Joyce countered that, due to temporal constraints, only a limited number of courtesy calls were possible in any given month, but that advertising, in essence, can act as a full-time sales agent, communicating with many more individuals than would be possible otherwise. She felt that if the billboard artwork was attractively designed and incorporated guidance supplied by the outdoor advertising industry, such as full color, high contrast, large text, few words, and so on, the billboards would have the potential to make a significant difference.

She went on to state that she believed that Brookwood should at least give billboards a chance. If they failed to deliver patients, the practice simply would refrain from their use in the future. But if they do deliver, Brookwood likely would witness considerable growth that might give it the upper hand in the battle for market share.

As for the specific focus of the billboard advertisement, Joyce believed that the panel should promote laser vision correction services. This was motivated by many things, but the main reason pertained to the fact that in Stanford, the market share battle was primarily waged on these particular services so it made sense for Brookwood to emphasize this in its billboard advertisements. She envisioned a very simple but colorful advertisement featuring Brookwood Vision Center's logo, street and Web site addresses, telephone number, and the tag line "laser vision correction."

After making her case, Dr. Thomas agreed reluctantly to fund the billboard campaign. He still was not convinced of the associated merit of the medium but perhaps Brookwood's experience with billboards would prove him otherwise. To assess the value of the billboard campaign, he instructed Joyce to devise a system of monitoring billboard effectiveness. She had already worked out a framework for doing just that by monitoring call volume, laser vision correction procedures, and by surveying patients to determine if they had noticed Brookwood's billboards.

One month after the billboards were posted, Dr. Thomas asked Joyce for a progress report. Joyce noted that, based on survey findings, patients were indeed noticing the billboards, but that few indicated that they were influenced to visit due to the advertisements. Further, Brookwood Vision Center had witnessed an increase in telephone inquiries asking for information on the advertised product, but patient volume directly attributable to the billboards was very minimal. Dr. Thomas responded that this was exactly what he expected, proclaiming that he knew that advertising did not work.

DISCUSSION

1. Dr. Thomas seems to believe that, after 30 days, Brookwood Vision Center's billboard advertising campaign is a failure. Thinking of the high-involvement nature of laser vision correction services, is Dr. Thomas' verdict premature? Why or why not?

2. At the conclusion of the case, we are left wondering how Joyce responded to Dr. Thomas' criticisms of advertising generally and the Brookwood billboard campaign specifically. If you were in Joyce's position, how would you have responded to Dr. Thomas?

3. Calculating return on investment for advertisements is very challenging, especially with billboards. What are your thoughts on Joyce's system for determining the effectiveness of Brookwood's billboard advertising campaign? What would you suggest to improve her system?

4. Joyce was compelled to use billboard advertising due to the medium's high reach and frequency and low cost point relative to other mass media. In your given market, investigate the costs of communicating with audiences via television, newspaper, and billboard advertising. Prepare a comparative analysis of the media using information from your investigation. What did you learn?

5. Joyce appeared to be following guidance provided by the outdoor advertising industry in designing Brookwood's billboard advertisement. For further insights and experience in the area of billboard advertising creativity, contact an outdoor advertising company in your local market and request advice on designing high-performing billboards. Then, tour your community for the purpose of examining posted billboards in an effort to ascertain compliance with creative guidance. What did you discover?

11

The Perfect Formula

SNAPSHOT

Institutions:

Pacific Cardiology, an established provider of cardiology services occupying the runner-up market share position in the city of Florence

Ridgewood Cardiology, an established provider of cardiology services occupying the position of market leader in the city of Florence

Metropolitan Cardiology, an out-of-market cardiology services provider

Location:

Florence (population 916,952), located in the New England region of the United States

Characters:

Mr. Arnold Christopher, Administrator
Dr. Richard Hernandez, Managing Partner and Cardiologist
(both of Pacific Cardiology)

Context:

In this case, a newly hired administrator of a cardiology clinic discovers that "sure things" in the area of marketing communications simply do not exist.

Arnold Christopher, Administrator of Pacific Cardiology, is confounded. With great confidence, he implemented his master marketing communications plan but the results were far less than stellar. This is particularly troubling to Arnold, as he was hired by Pacific Cardiology primarily on his proven ability to attract new customers as demonstrated in a previous employment experience. But 9 months into his opportunity at Pacific Cardiology, he cannot seem to generate any significant gains in patient volume. The pressure to deliver results is now higher than ever, but he is at a loss as his plan seems to have failed. He does not know what to do.

Pacific Cardiology is a prominent cardiology services provider, consisting of 11 physician partner/owners, which is located in the city of Florence (population 916,952) situated in the New England region of the United States. The for-profit establishment has generated a loyal following of patients over its 12-year history, acquiring a fairly large share of the market. The physicians, however, have their sights set on market leadership and need to win new customers to capture the position that is now held by arch rival, Ridgewood Cardiology, the cardiology services division of Ridgewood Health System.

Arnold is no stranger to medical practice management, as he managed a very similar practice in another state, Metropolitan Cardiology. There, he earned the reputation of marketing guru, courtesy of his success at building market share. In less than 2 years, Arnold moved Metropolitan Cardiology from third place to market leader, garnering him much praise. The secret of Arnold's success at market-share building centered on his ability to design a marketing communications plan that actually worked. Over many months of trial and error, Arnold fine-tuned the marketing communications mix deployed by Metropolitan Cardiology to create what he believed to be the answer for generating high levels of attention and enticing patronage.

Arnold called his plan the 3-2-1 because he called on three advertising media (i.e., television, radio, and outdoor), two public relations techniques (i.e., facility tours and educational seminars both promoted via press release), and one sales promotion technique (i.e., free gifts carrying the company logo that were distributed to patients and other parties). He had experimented with both personal selling and direct marketing but found them to deliver undesirable results. Hence, he called on three of the traditional five components of the marketing communications mix.

Although it took Arnold about a year to perfect his formula for success, the wait was worth it as Metropolitan Cardiology began seeing the results almost immediately. The formula was obviously on target and it propelled Arnold's career to new heights, ultimately leading to his new opportunity at Pacific Cardiology.

Thinking that he had found the secret formula for success, Arnold simply transferred his 3-2-1 marketing communications framework to the Florence market. Emboldened by his prior successes, he gambled his entire annual marketing budget at Pacific Cardiology on this approach, believing that the 3-2-1 marketing communications plan worked universally.

At the end of the campaign's first month, aggregate patient encounters were identical to the same period in the prior year, although surveys indicated a heightened awareness of Pacific Cardiology among both current and new patients. Arnold was not concerned as he knew that it would take time for the marketing communications to deliver desired results. As Arnold watched the second and third months of the Pacific Cardiology campaign pass, patient encounters continued to be flat. Arnold continued to believe in his plan, but by the sixth month of similar patient traffic, he became concerned that his formula was off-the-mark.

The lack of results did not go unnoticed by the partner/owners of Pacific Cardiology. Just after the 6-month point, Arnold was called into a meeting with Dr. Richard Hernandez, Managing Partner, who pressured him for an explanation. Being that Arnold was hired primarily on his proven ability to increase patient traffic, Dr. Hernandez conveyed that he and his colleagues felt as though enough time had passed for them to see results. They were demanding action.

Anticipating such criticisms, Arnold already had planned his response, assuring Dr. Hernandez that marketing communications take time to generate patronage and that the results witnessed at this point were to be expected. He continued on, stating that consumers must first gain an awareness of a given product upon which, when a want or need arises, they will be more likely to forward their patronage due to their associated knowledge. To the campaign's credit, Arnold pointed out the heightened awareness in the marketplace, which he believed would lead to increased patronage over time. Arnold then requested patience and communicated that he was confident that the second half of the campaign would yield the results desired by all. Dr. Hernandez was apprehensive but, on hearing Arnold's justifications, he believed that results would be forthcoming and advocated a continuation of the marketing communications campaign.

Although Arnold outwardly conveyed confidence in his ability to deliver patients, inwardly he was beginning to panic. A nurse by training, he never received any formal education in administration, acquiring associated skills on-the-job. But now his lack of expertise is beginning to show as he does not know what to do or if he should do anything at all. He began to doubt both his experience and his 3-2-1 plan, thinking that perhaps his prior marketing successes resulted simply from luck.

Arnold joined Pacific Cardiology with great confidence, believing that his 3-2-1 plan would work in Florence just as it worked at Metropolitan Cardiology. He believed that he had done his homework, intensively studying the two cities, learning that they were virtually identical in terms of geographic, demographic, and sociocultural attributes. He assumed that this would permit a direct transferal of the 3-2-1 plan with similar, if not identical, results, but this clearly was not the case.

Arnold decided to continue to believe in his 3-2-1 plan despite clear indications that the plan was not delivering desired results. He had exhausted his marketing budget anyway, making it impossible for him to change his course of action. Further, he had too much pride to admit to the partner/owners of Pacific Cardiology that both he and his plan were in distress.

At the 9-month point, market share had not budged. Pacific Cardiology continued to be in second place, trailing Ridgewood Cardiology by the same margin as when Arnold had initiated his 3-2-1 plan. Arnold now has resigned himself to the fact that the plan is a failure and has realized that his tenure with Pacific Cardiology is severely threatened. Although he has achieved other victories on behalf of the practice in various areas of administration and overall operations, he knew that he was primarily hired for the purpose of bringing Pacific Cardiology into a position of market leadership. As the days pass by, Arnold feels increasingly uneasy and he has no idea which direction he should take, either personally or professionally.

DISCUSSION

1. Arnold is panicked that his 3-2-1 marketing communications plan is not delivering customers. He has indications that the plan is increasing awareness of Pacific Cardiology in the marketplace, but 9 months into the campaign, patient visits have not budged and the practice remains locked in second place, failing to make any advances on the market leadership position. Should Arnold be panicked? Why or why not?

2. Arnold has resigned himself to the fact that his 3-2-1 marketing communications plan is not working and he seems to be blaming the plan itself for the lack of results. But many issues potentially could be impacting the performance of his plan. Although the case does not provide enough information to make such determinations, what factors have the potential to negatively impact even the best laid marketing communications plans, rendering little, if any, gains in the marketplace?

3. At the 6-month point, Dr. Hernandez, on behalf of his fellow partner/owners, communicated growing impatience with the lackluster results of Arnold's marketing communications plan. Privately, Arnold began to panic and did not know which course of action to take. Ultimately, he decided to continue down the current path, not making any alterations to his plan. If you were Arnold, what action would you have taken at the 6-month point and why? How would you have addressed the concerns expressed by Dr. Hernandez?

4. After his success at Metropolitan Cardiology, Arnold believed that he had discovered the secret formula for marketing communications success, but that formula seemed not to work equally well when deployed by Pacific Cardiology. Arnold was dumbfounded by this, especially given the parallel nature of the two markets. What lessons does this teach us about marketing communications?

5. While Arnold might not have been successful at identifying the secret formula for marketing communications success, are there, in fact, any formulas that marketers can turn to for guaranteed success? Think deeply on the discipline and its marketing communications component and report your insights.

Finding the Right Mix

Lea Ann Gibson, Director of Marketing for Highland Hospital, has finally found the solution to a problem she has been facing for the better part of a year. Specifically, she has discovered the right marketing communications mix for the hospital's under-construction assisted-living center. It took months of trial and error, caused many sleepless nights for her, and had negative implications for at least one employee, but she is now receiving inquiries from interested parties seeking to lease assisted-living units, whereas there was nearly complete silence before. Lea Ann is able now to breathe a sigh of relief.

This all began approximately 1 year ago, when the decision was made by Bob Jefferson, Highland Hospital's Administrator, and the establishment's governing board to construct an assisted-living center, following months of studies to assess community need and economic feasibility. The project was approved and Lea Ann was given the responsibility of leasing its 40 units.

Highland Hospital is a 60-bed, not-for-profit provider of general medical and surgical services. Based in the small city of Hazlehurst (population 21,204) located in the New England region of the United States, the hospital provides a valuable service to its residents. The city is situated approximately 40 miles from a much larger, metropolitan area, anchored by Monroe, a city of 249,775 residents. Hazlehurst historically has served as a somewhat independent community, where people worked, lived, and shopped without circulating to outside communities, but in recent years, it has become more of a commuter city for Monroe and its surrounding suburbs, something hastened by improvements in transportation and thriving economic development occurring in and around Monroe. The urban sprawl centered on Monroe prompted many to relocate to Hazlehurst, as it is a more family-friendly community, something that has benefited every business in the city, including Highland Hospital.

Given the demographics of the region, coupled with Hazlehurst's quality of life and quick access to Monroe, it seemed logical for Highland Hospital to enter the assisted-living marketplace. Across the region, there were very few assisted-living centers, making Highland Hospital one of the first in the area to offer these services. Further, the hospital could tap not only the needs of the population of Hazlehurst, but also the needs of Monroe and surrounding suburbs, given their close proximity. The new property, being constructed adjacent to Highland Hospital, was named Highland Park.

Lea Ann was excited about the opportunities associated with marketing a brand new product for Highland Hospital and was tasked with formulating the marketing communications mix in a manner that would attract the attention of target audiences and ultimately result in leased units. Construction of the rather elaborate facility was anticipated to take 12 months, giving her ample time to lease units prior to its official grand opening. Lea Ann set the goal of having all 40 units leased by Highland Park's formal introduction into the market.

Given Highland Hospital's very small size, Lea Ann was forced to work with an equally small marketing budget for the promotion of Highland Park. The tiny budget essentially meant that Lea Ann had to make the right decisions on her selection of given marketing communications vehicles that would be deployed. Any misstep and she would not have marketing resources to fall back on, raising the stakes of her associated decisions. The budget, in fact, was too small to spread over myriad types of communications, so it was imperative for her to select a small number of communication avenues and funnel resources down those pathways accordingly, hoping that the given selections would successfully attract patronage.

Lea Ann began by examining the traditional marketing communications mix of advertising, personal selling, sales promotion, public relations, and direct marketing. She knew that it would be essential to have brochures and other sales materials, so she decided to include direct marketing in her given mix. The brochures could be used onsite, being distributed to interested parties, and also could be posted to target audiences as direct mail pieces. Public relations, of course, would be deployed as the preparation and submission of press releases and the conduct of facility and model residential unit tours could be effected at little or no cost. Sales promotion was viewed by Lea Ann to be a luxury rather than a necessity and was ruled out.

The selections were fairly simple up until Lea Ann faced decisions regarding advertising and personal selling. The amount of advertising required to communicate with desired audiences would be very expensive, just as would the hiring of a sales representative who would be tasked with promoting Highland Park both on-and-off site. Debating the two options, Lea Ann knew that her limited resource pool would require selection of one or the other. Having concerns that she could not build up the critical mass of advertising required to engage desired audiences with her given budget, she opted to go with personal selling instead. This required the hiring of a sales representative for Highland Park, whom she intended to call a leasing agent. This person would be responsible for a mixture of outside sales, by calling on interested individuals and organizations in the region, and inside sales, by conducting tours of the model residential unit and other on-premises presentations designed to facilitate leasing. Lea Ann viewed this approach to be less risky than advertising. It also included the benefit of adding labor for the many on-site tasks associated with leasing residential units at Highland Park.

Satisfied with her plan, Lea Ann met with Bob and presented her marketing communications mix that called on personal selling, direct marketing, and public relations. Bob concurred with Lea Ann's recommendations and authorized her to proceed. Over the coming weeks, Lea Ann prepared direct mail materials, designed public relations templates and associated ideas for generating publicity for Highland Park, and interviewed applicants for the new leasing position, eventually hiring Kimberly Lancaster for the role.

As Kimberly was a key to the leasing campaign's success, Lea Ann took great care to orient her to the Highland Park construction plan, the model residential unit, and appropriate marketing strategies and tactics. She also worked with her to arrange presentations at various civic clubs, professional organizations, and senior citizen gatherings, hoping to spread the word about Highland Park. With only 10 months remaining before Highland Park's grand opening, time was of the essence, but given Kimberly's prior experience as a successful pharmaceutical sales representative, Lea Ann had confidence that she could indeed sell Highland Park.

Two months later, Kimberly clearly was making the rounds in the community and beyond, conducting approximately 10 formal presentations per week and holding numerous informal meetings with target audiences, yet no residential units had been leased. Lea Ann was not overly concerned, given that she understood that it would take time for the leasing efforts to pay off. There still was plenty of time left to lease the residential units, but Lea Ann was somewhat troubled by the lack of inquiries generated by the various presentations held by Kimberly. Almost no telephone traffic had resulted.

Two more months pass, with it now being only 6 months away from the grand opening. Still, Kimberly's efforts had not resulted in the leasing of a single residential unit. Further, very few inquiries were being forwarded.

Given the lackluster results, Lea Ann began to realize that personal selling was not the correct approach for leasing Highland Park's residential units. Something had to change.

After considerable debate, Lea Ann made the decision to terminate Kimberly. This was most unfortunate, but essential as it permitted Lea Ann to direct the money that would have gone toward Kimberly's salary toward advertising. With her budget freed up, time running out, and massive pressure from Bob and the governing board, Lea Ann knew that this was her last chance. She decided to gamble on television advertisements and, with a very limited budget, decided to run the advertisements only during local newscasts on Monroe's three local television stations, which reached far beyond the city into Hazlehurst and beyond. Lea Ann knew that local newscasts had high viewership, even among those who do not normally watch television, and, while costs were higher during these telecasts, so too was reach. To extend the temporal length of the advertising campaign and create the perception of more robust message dissemination, Lea Ann rotated the campaign from one station to another on a weekly basis. A single Highland Park television advertisement was produced very inexpensively by the production crew of one of Monroe's television stations and used across all given stations.

Highland Park's television advertising campaign immediately ensued and within 1 week, Lea Ann had received more inquiries than in the entire 6 month period preceding the television advertisements. Lea Ann breathed a sigh of relief.

DISCUSSION

1. Lea Ann learned that personal selling was ineffective for enticing target audiences to lease residential units at Highland Park, yet television advertisements seemed to be effective. Although the case does not provide enough details to make a certain determination, why might the television advertisements have been more effective at reaching audiences and prompting inquiries than that of personal selling?

2. Although personal selling did not work well for Highland Park, do you see any merit in deploying this form of marketing communication in similar contexts, that is, when resources are very low? Why or why not?

3. What are your thoughts on the approach to television advertising used by Lea Ann, that is, to run the Highland Park advertisements only during local newscasts? In your local market, what results would you expect to achieve from this approach?

4. Using a standard marketing or advertising textbook, investigate advertising scheduling patterns and identify the given pattern used by Lea Ann in Highland Park's television advertising campaign. Do you think the scheduling pattern used by Lea Ann is best or would you have preferred a different scheduling pattern in this situation? Be sure to provide your associated rationale.

5. Why do you think marketing communications work in some situations and not in others, even when deployed in seemingly identical environments with seemingly identical target audiences? What does this say about the difficulties inherent in formulating the marketing communications mix?

13

Covert Operations

SNAPSHOT

Institution:
Renew Clinic, a three-physician medical practice specializing in cosmetic surgery

Location:
Brookhaven (population 437,319), located in the South Atlantic region of the United States

Characters:
Dr. Gene Cole, Co-Owner and Cosmetic Surgeon
Dr. William Shelton, Co-Owner and Cosmetic Surgeon
Dr. Margaret Steel, Co-Owner and Cosmetic Surgeon
Ms. Emily Bryant, Marketing Agent (and patient)
(all of Renew Clinic)

Context:
In this case, the physician–owners of a cosmetic surgery clinic resort to a highly controversial marketing communications method to increase patient volume.

Dr. Gene Cole has a crafty idea. Specifically, he plans to introduce a very controversial method for communicating with target audiences, one that even has ethical implications. Dr. Cole has spoken with his two physician partners, Drs. William Shelton and Margaret Steel, and they have agreed to brush aside ethical considerations, opting instead to use what is definitely a very risky marketing communications technique on the belief that it will deliver customers to their cosmetic surgery practice, which is thirsting for increased patient volume.

Dr. Cole is a co-owner of and cosmetic surgeon for Renew Clinic, a three-physician cosmetic surgery practice based in the city of Brookhaven (population 437,319), situated in the South Atlantic region of the United States. The 12-year-old practice, not unlike that of many cosmetic surgery practices located across the country, is engaged in heated competition for the cosmetic surgery dollars of consumers in the marketplace. While demand for cosmetic surgery services is increasing in Brookhaven, so too is supply, with new practices appearing seemingly overnight, further squeezing the ability of established practices to maintain viable patient populations. This has created an ultra-competitive environment with clinics fighting for market share, most typically by deploying an extensive range of marketing communications in ongoing attempts to attract and retain target audiences.

Indeed, cosmetic surgery providers alone account for a sizeable portion of the marketing communications investment in the city, making them a defined favorite client of advertising agencies and media companies of all kinds, as they are locked into ever-escalating marketing communications purchases as practices work to outdo each other. To attract customers, cosmetic surgery practices in Brookhaven heavily look to the traditional marketing communications mix, deploying advertising across all media categories; engaging in direct marketing efforts, with direct mail pieces being the mainstay; managing public relations, with press releases announcing newsworthy items in an effort a garner media attention; tapping into sales promotion by distributing free gifts to patients and other publics; and even calling on personal selling by fielding sales agents who visit area establishments to discuss the various services of their given practices.

Campaigns span the gamut of style and substance, with some cosmetic surgery practices deploying very dignified, professional marketing communications campaigns and others pushing the envelope of good taste, especially when promoting services such as breast augmentation. The occurrence of practices that resort to less tasteful tactics is increasing and is indicative of a highly competitive marketplace where some practices feel the need to resort to more aggressive, over-the-top campaigns to garner higher levels of attention in hopes of attracting patrons. Renew Clinic has always taken the high road, deploying marketing communications campaigns that are tasteful depictions of the services that the practice provides for the purpose of enhancing one's body.

While Renew Clinic possesses a viable population of patients, its three physicians are hungry for more, with hopes of achieving additional growth, yielding more income and prestige. In seeking to find a pathway to that growth, Dr. Cole set out to examine what might be done. He first considered increasing the marketing communications purchases of the practice, but on further review, he believed that Renew Clinic's promotions efforts had reached the point of saturation, yielding diminishing returns for each additional marketing communication dollar spent. He also feared that more robust purchases would simply be matched by competitors, ultimately serving to increase marketing communications expenditures with no improvement in market share.

Not satisfied, Dr. Cole continued his pursuit of a growth pathway, eventually happening upon the idea of stealth marketing, which involves the use of sales agents who patronize various venues, such as bars or other public gathering spots, for the purpose of promoting given products to target audiences. However, unlike traditional sales representatives who disclose that they are employed by given firms, stealth marketing agents do not disclose that they have a business interest in the companies that produce or provide the particular promoted items, making them seem to simply be providing word-of-mouth referrals, rather than paid sales pitches. This gives the recommendations of stealth marketers enhanced credibility, as consumers generally have a higher opinion of unpaid, word-of-mouth referrals than paid forms of communication. Stealth marketing, which goes by many names, including undercover marketing, is considered by many to be deceptive as sales agents make no mention of, and in fact overtly hide, their relationships with given employers. The consumer is oblivious to the true relationship between agent and company and becomes the unwitting target of what is essentially a camouflaged sales pitch. Although stealth marketing seemed to be sinister to Dr. Cole, especially given Renew Clinic's history of taking the high road in its various marketing communications efforts, the battle for market share was very real and demanded action. Dr. Cole decided to craft an associated plan.

Thinking of recent patients who might have the ability to serve as a test subject for Renew Clinic's stealth marketing trial, he recalled Emily Bryant, a 21-year-old college student who recently presented for breast augmentation and liposuction. Emily was a very attractive woman who had an engaging and magnetic personality. Her cosmetic treatments further enhanced her beauty, making her hard to miss, especially in social situations where less formal attire is the rule, rather than the exception.

In casual discussions occurring as Dr. Cole went about effecting Emily's various cosmetic procedures, he observed a very sociable person who enjoyed living life to the fullest. Emily regularly discussed her participation in Brookhaven's burgeoning club scene, giving her access to a wealth of potential customers for the medical practice. She also was heavily involved in athletics, both in the community and at her university. She was the perfect stealth marketing candidate.

Working through the details of his plan, Dr. Cole envisioned Emily serving as Renew Clinic's stealth marketing agent, where she would be required to visit a defined number of social venues on a weekly basis for the purpose of surreptitiously promoting the practice to patrons of given establishments. Specifically, Emily would socialize, just as she normally would do in such environments, but work to direct the conversations toward beauty, casually bringing up the role that Renew Clinic played in assisting her in the quest for physical perfection. Of course, she would never mention her affiliation with Renew Clinic as its sales agent, but instead would present herself as one who had such a great experience as a patient that she felt compelled to let others know about the care and results provided by the practice. When targets seemed especially interested, Emily would "just happen" to have a Renew Clinic business card on hand, requesting that she be mentioned as the referring party.

Dr. Cole believed that Emily could stealthily sell the services of Renew Clinic at bars, concerts, swimming pool parties, and related social events, seeking to direct conversations down a pathway that led to discussions that prompted mention of the cosmetic surgery practice. Her compensation might perhaps consist of a base salary, a commission for referrals, and reimbursement for the costs associated with her social activities, including cover charges, bar tabs, memberships, and so on. Emily, of course, would be required to maintain complete confidentiality regarding her employment and she would need quite a bit of coaching to ensure that the stealth marketing efforts conducted on behalf of Renew Clinic were indeed stealth and remained that way.

Dr. Cole presented his idea and working plan to Drs. Shelton and Steel. While all three of the cosmetic surgeons viewed this to be an extremely risky endeavor and had many ethical concerns over its use, they agreed that a trial should be conducted. With authorization, Dr. Cole contacted Emily and asked her to visit the practice to learn of an exciting opportunity. On her arrival at Renew Clinic, the three physicians discussed her participation in the practice's newest effort to capture market share. Without any hesitation, Emily accepted.

DISCUSSION

1. Drs. Cole, Shelton, and Steel have decided to pursue stealth marketing as a means of increasing patronage at Renew Clinic. Ethical considerations aside, what are your thoughts on this technique's potential as a marketing communications device? What are the pitfalls of this approach? What, for example, might happen if Emily was discovered to be working for Renew Clinic? Do you believe that Renew Clinic is selling out, given its historic approach to marketing communications? Please explain your responses.

2. In an effort to stimulate growth, Dr. Cole considered increasing the budget of current marketing communications devices, but opted against doing so as he believed this to be futile, likely resulting in escalation with no real market share victories. He also had concerns regarding diminishing returns. What are your thoughts on his perspectives? Are his views accurate? Why or why not?

3. Assume that Renew Clinic has asked you for assistance in formalizing a plan for Emily to pursue in her stealth marketing endeavors? Using your local community as the target market for Renew Clinic, prepare a detailed schedule for Emily, indicating places for her to visit and approaches to use in each venue over the course of a 1-month period.

4. This case presents the consideration and ultimate use of stealth marketing in a cosmetic surgery practice; however, many other types of healthcare entities exist. Select five different types of healthcare entities and discuss how stealth marketing might be deployed in each. Do some healthcare organizations better lend themselves to stealth marketing than others? Why or why not?

5. Do you believe that stealth marketing is ethical? Why or why not?

14

Form or Function

Amanda Connors, newly hired Chief Marketing Officer at Evergreen Hospital, is excited. She has just moved into an organization that, in her opinion, has been deploying some of the most boring advertisements ever created. Drawing on her education and experience in the creative arts, she is looking forward to adding some flash and style to Evergreen Hospital's advertisements, elevating the aesthetic appeal of its promotional messages and gaining recognition both for the hospital and for herself.

Evergreen Hospital is a 250-bed, for-profit provider of general medical and surgical services located in Louisville, a city of 357,465 situated in the Pacific region of the United States. Well operated and financially sound, the hospital has been the benefactor of a well-run marketing department, headed by a skilled executive, Simon Davidson, who recently retired.

Simon was formally trained in marketing, possessing Bachelor's and Master's degrees in the discipline. Through Simon's efforts over his 20-year career, Evergreen Hospital emerged as a healthcare powerhouse, becoming one of the top three providers in the marketplace in an environment that remains highly competitive. While Evergreen Hospital was saddened to see Simon retire, the establishment is very pleased that Amanda will be taking the helm, expecting to see continued excellence in marketing.

Unlike Simon, Amanda possesses credentials that are outside of the formal discipline of marketing, but are closely related, namely a Bachelor's Degree in Creative Arts and a Master's Degree in Mass Communications. Although she has never held a formal marketing management position, she has served in numerous positions in advertising agencies, most recently serving as a senior executive at one of the largest in Louisville. Given Amanda's vast experience in advertising, Walter Franklin, Evergreen's Chief Executive Officer, extended an offer to her for the position of Chief Marketing Officer, which she gladly accepted.

Welcoming the new opportunity, Amanda believes that she possesses the ability to advance the hospital on multiple marketing fronts, but she views advertising to be the area that she will most heavily influence; an understandable perspective given her background and experience. After a brief orientation, Amanda is given free reign to operate the department as she sees fit.

Over the years, Amanda has observed Evergreen Hospital's advertisements and has always believed that they lacked true creativity. The very basic messages and creative treatments that were typical in Evergreen's promotional messages left a lot to be desired by someone who had a true flair for graphic design and artistic direction. Amanda believed that Evergreen Hospital was missing out on opportunities as a result of its very conservative advertisements. Therefore, her first order of business was to shake things up, breathing life into what she viewed to be staid creativity.

Wanting to score an early victory to demonstrate her value to the hospital, Amanda worked feverishly on the assembly of an integrated marketing communications campaign that incorporated her special touch. She decided to deploy billboards, magazine advertisements, and direct mail pieces, each carrying a unique creative treatment that was far removed from previous efforts at Evergreen Hospital.

Specifically, Amanda worked to design a transformational campaign, abandoning the informational campaigns that were historically deployed by Evergreen Hospital. Her efforts resulted in what she referred to as the "FEEL" campaign. This involved the use of the word "FEEL" prominently displayed in large, uppercase, bold text as the central feature of given advertisements. Much smaller, lowercase text in contrasting colors, offset to the bottom right of the word "FEEL,' was used to create inventive messages, yielding advertisements that read "FEEL better," "FEEL well," "FEEL at peace," and so on, illustrating improved states of health and wellness. Artistic textures were used as backdrops, rounded out by a very small Evergreen Hospital logo which was placed in the far upper right corner of the particular advertisements. Amanda was very proud of her work.

Seeking feedback, Amanda circulated mock-ups of the advertisements to Evergreen's senior managers. Everyone was extremely impressed by the campaign, which appeared to be more of an artistic display than a promotional endeavor and definitely prompted reflection regarding the associated meaning of the advertisements. Without hesitation, Walter directed Amanda to initiate the campaign immediately.

As a new month ushers in, so too does the "FEEL" campaign. Feedback from Amanda's former colleagues in the advertising industry was brisk, with everyone congratulating her on infusing true art for the first time into Evergreen's advertisements. The compliments kept coming over the weeks and months of the campaign, with perhaps the most flattering one being her campaign's nomination for, and later receipt of, a local advertising award. Amanda was ecstatic, relishing in the glory and enjoying the praise she received from her fellow employees of Evergreen Hospital and various publics.

A number of months later, Amanda set out to craft a follow-up campaign, knowing that the "FEEL" campaign soon would need to be replaced to prevent the onset of advertising wearout where audiences begin to grow accustomed to, and less receptive of, long-running campaigns. As she began brainstorming on the future campaign, Walter telephoned her and asked her to step over to his office.

On Amanda's arrival at Walter's office, she found him reviewing the latest patient volume and market share figures. She anticipated great things given the notoriety of the "FEEL" campaign, but much to her surprise, Walter informed her that patient volume was down across many service lines and that Evergreen Hospital was losing ground in the battle for market share. Although he did not voice his opinion months earlier when Amanda initiated a more creative approach to Evergreen Hospital's advertising initiatives via the "FEEL" campaign, Walter communicated that he did have concerns in the back of his mind that the campaign was focused too much on art and too little on selling healthcare services.

Walter went on to state that, both institutionally and environmentally, the only substantive change in the preceding months pertained to the major shift in the direction of Evergreen's marketing efforts, namely its advertisements, leading him to believe that they were the culprit that was causing declining business performance. He noted that while the informational campaigns deployed by Evergreen Hospital in years past might have seemed bland to art enthusiasts and creative professionals, they conveyed very practical, tastefully designed messages that undoubtedly drove business. Walter indicated that he was very much willing to pursue a different, more creative, transformational approach, but that he now has concerns that this method is inappropriate for Evergreen Hospital. Walter suggested to Amanda that she direct attention to the formulation and implementation of a more balanced campaign that emphasized selling first and creativity second. Amanda was crushed.

DISCUSSION

1. Amanda's advertising approach represented a radical departure from that embraced by Simon, yet Simon had been very successful using his approach to build market share over a 20-year period at Evergreen Hospital. Given that Evergreen Hospital's advertisements under Simon's leadership had been successful at building market share, should Walter have been more hesitant when he authorized Amanda to take the hospital's advertising in a new direction? Why or why not?

2. In the case, Walter makes the assumption that Evergreen Hospital's reduced patient volume and declining market share resulted from Amanda's deployment of very different advertisements that were emphasizing art over sales. He bases this assumption on the fact that, both institutionally and environmentally, the only substantive change in the preceding months pertained to a major shift in Evergreen's advertising. Amanda appears to have no counter argument, indicating that she likely had not been assessing return on investment. What mechanisms could she have instituted to measure campaign performance, potentially giving her an argument to counter Walter's criticisms?

3. This case illustrates the battle that occasionally occurs between creative professionals and marketing professionals, with creative types often emphasizing art elements over sales elements and marketing types often emphasizing sales elements over art elements. Who should win this battle and why?

4. It certainly is possible to strike a balance between art and sales elements, yielding effective advertisements, but extremes often result when one side or the other runs wild. Taking the medium of billboard advertising, tour your local market and identify one example of an art-heavy billboard, a sales-heavy billboard, and a balanced billboard. Prepare a narrative describing your rationale for classifying the billboards as you did. If possible, take photographs of your selections. In your opinion, which approach will yield the best business results for healthcare entities?

5. Aside from the obvious issue pertaining to varying philosophies of advertising, this case addresses the more general issue of the risk associated with altering proven strategic directions. At Evergreen Hospital, the establishment had been witnessing positive business results courtesy of Simon's approach to advertising, but began to experience declines when Amanda's approach was implemented. What would motivate one to abandon a given course of action that has been proven to be successful and what are the risks associated with doing so? What is your philosophy regarding the alteration of proven courses of action?

CHAPTER 15

The Public
Relations Disaster

SNAPSHOT

Institution:
Lakeland Hospital, a 275-bed, for-profit establishment offering general medical and surgical services

Location:
Jackson (population 350,759), located in the Middle Atlantic region of the United States

Characters:
Ms. Katherine Bennett, Chief Marketing Officer
Mr. Arthur Rooney, Chief Executive Officer
Dr. William Smith, Physician
(all of Lakeland Hospital)

Context:
In this case, a hospital decides to feature one of its physicians in its advertisements and all seems well until domestic violence charges are filed against the caregiver.

Katherine Bennett, Chief Marketing Officer at Lakeland Hospital, thought she had seen it all—until now. The hospital has been running advertisements in recent weeks and months that feature its own employees. The advertisements have generated much attention because they present familiar faces in the community, but in recent days, the level of attention directed to Lakeland Hospital's advertisements has reached a fever pitch. Normally, this would be a good thing, but given the reason behind the attention, it is something that Katherine would much prefer to do without.

Much to Katherine's horror, earlier in the week, she learned that the employee featured in this month's advertisements, Dr. William Smith, was arrested on domestic violence charges. In an effort to help Lakeland Hospital save face, Katherine took immediate action to reel in the advertisements featuring Dr. Smith, but this has proven to be more complicated than she had ever imagined.

Lakeland Hospital is a 275-bed, for-profit medical facility located in Jackson, a city of 350,759 residents in the Middle Atlantic region of the United States. The hospital was established 25 years ago and is known for its cutting edge technology, excellent staff, high-quality medical care, and, thanks to Katherine, innovative advertising campaigns.

Katherine joined Lakeland Hospital 4 years ago after a decade of service as the Creative Director for a local advertising agency. Once at the helm of marketing operations at Lakeland Hospital, she greatly modified the hospital's advertising approach. Specifically, she introduced a less corporate-oriented, more personal, local touch to creative treatments and displays. The result was very well received in the community and even garnered a few local advertising awards.

Some months ago when Katherine decided to feature actual employees in advertisements, Arthur Rooney, Lakeland Hospital's Chief Executive Officer, was hesitant, but later became supportive of the initiative on Katherine's assurances. Indeed, many positive things resulted from the very personal advertisements. For example, employees were very excited to see their colleagues featured in the various marketing communications. Family members and other community publics also were impressed, because it placed a more personal face on Lakeland Hospital.

Katherine was a mastermind of integrated marketing communications and she deployed a comprehensive range of communicative mechanisms to gain the attention of target markets. Her specific communications mix included advertising, with television, radio, newspaper, and billboard advertisements being used extensively; direct marketing, with direct mail being the primary communication mechanism; public relations, with press releases being used effectively to announce critical events at Lakeland Hospital; and sales promotion, with a range of contests being offered periodically to generate attention.

Everything had been going so well, at least until Katherine woke up Monday morning, turned on her television to watch the local news, and saw Dr. Smith being handcuffed and placed in a police car, arrested on the charge of domestic abuse. Dr. Smith posted bail and was released from custody later in the day, once again followed by television cameras and news reporters eager to get the latest details. Hoping to catch of glimpse of the well-known physician, press trucks were even camped in front of both Dr. Smith's house and Lakeland Hospital, providing perfect backdrops for live newscasts on the latest high-profile controversy in Jackson.

The bad situation was made even worse due to the nature of Lakeland Hospital's advertisements featuring Dr. Smith. Specifically, the television and radio advertisements featured the physician discussing the care and concern that he and his colleagues deliver at Lakeland Hospital—not the best of lines for one facing domestic violence charges. Further, the billboard advertisements prominently featured his photograph, along with the tagline, "Place your health in our caring hands," Lakeland Hospital's current promotional slogan.

Racing to put a halt to what had become a public relations nightmare, Katherine immediately telephoned her television and radio advertising sales representatives and was successful at having the advertisements featuring Dr. Smith immediately removed, substituting other Lakeland Hospital advertisements in their place. However, on contacting her outdoor advertising account representative, Katherine learned that the billboards could not be removed for another 3 days, the quickest the outdoor advertising company could dispatch a posting crew. Thankfully, no other marketing communications of Lakeland Hospital featured Dr. Smith, but the damage to the institution was already done.

After addressing Lakeland Hospital's advertisements, Katherine turned her attention to handling numerous news media requests seeking comments regarding the employment status of Dr. Smith and other aspects of his service at Lakeland Hospital. Working with Arthur, the two prepared a brief statement communicating that the issue pertaining to Dr. Smith was a personnel matter and that Lakeland Hospital does not comment on personnel matters. At that point, Katherine had done everything possible to stem the crisis, but she knew that more actions would need to be taken in coming days and weeks.

As Katherine's very long day came to a close, she reflected on the damage done to the image of Lakeland Hospital. Even though Dr. Smith is innocent until proven guilty, the ramifications of the allegations against him are far reaching, extending to Lakeland Hospital—a matter made worse by the advertisements which prominently featured the physician. A 6 PM newscast even used one of Lakeland Hospital's billboards featuring Dr. Smith as a backdrop to report on the story.

The next morning, Arthur called Katherine into his office to discuss the marketing implications of the matter. He specifically informed Katherine that Lakeland Hospital will need to rethink its advertising approach. Arthur further conveyed that his initial reservations with featuring employees in Lakeland Hospital's advertisements stemmed from his concerns regarding the unknown. He went on to provide a few examples, noting that employees featured in Lakeland Hospital's advertisements might possibly resign, immediately rendering given advertisements obsolete. Arthur asked Katherine what she would do if Lakeland Hospital spent thousands of dollars on advertisements featuring a particular employee, only to have the employee quit and go to work for a competing organization. She had no response.

Arthur then mentioned that the worst-case scenario and his greatest fear was that a featured employee would encounter trouble with the law, something that now had ultimately been realized. He went on to communicate that it was impossible for Lakeland Hospital to know everything about the personal lives of employees and that this made featuring them in advertisements a risky endeavor, something Katherine knows all too well now.

As Katherine made her way back to her office, she admitted to herself that she had never really considered the downside of featuring employees in advertisements. Still in damage-control mode, she began the day's work but wondered in the back of her mind what advertising approach she would turn to next.

DISCUSSION

1. This case presents a very negative consequence resulting from the use of a healthcare organization's own employees in its advertisements. What lessons does this case provide for those healthcare institutions using or considering the use of employees in their advertisements?

2. Erring on the side of caution, Arthur communicated to Katherine that a new advertising approach at Lakeland Hospital is needed,

effectively bringing to a close the highly personal, well-regarded approach initiated by Katherine that featured Lakeland Hospital's employees. Do you think Arthur is correct in his decision to abandon this particular approach? Why or why not?

3. Assume that Arthur backs away from his position and permits Katherine to continue featuring employees in Lakeland Hospital's advertisements. What mechanisms, if any, could be put into place to ensure that another incident like the one pertaining to Dr. Smith would not occur again? Are there any safeguards that come to mind to increase the likelihood that public relations disasters will not result from such personal approaches to advertising? Please explain your response.

4. Regarding featuring employees in advertisements, Arthur communicated to Katherine that the unknown was very troubling to him. He noted the presence of significant risks, such as the featured employee who quits and goes to work for a competitor or the featured employee who encounters legal troubles, as did Dr. Smith. But there are many other circumstances in which featured employees might cast an equally negative light on their healthcare institutions. What other circumstances come to mind?

5. While the case discusses featuring employees in the advertisements of healthcare institutions, there are other possibilities for personalization, one of which involves featuring actual patients in the advertisements. Make a detailed list of the positive and negative aspects associated with this practice. Would you recommend that hospitals and other healthcare providers feature their own patients in advertisements? Why or why not?

16

Tragedy of Tragedies

SNAPSHOT

Institutions:
Eastover Medical Center, a 290-bed, for-profit establishment providing general medical and surgical services
Eastover Wellness, a comprehensive wellness center owned and operated by Eastover Medical Center

Location:
Pinehurst (population 229,121), located in the Pacific region of the United States

Characters:
Ms. Rachel McIntyre, Director of Physical Therapy and Rehabilitative Services
Ms. Susan Norton, President and Chief Executive Officer
Ms. Theresa O'Connor, Physical Therapist and Part-Time Aerobics Instructor
(all of Eastover Medical Center)
Mr. Brian Rollins, former boyfriend of Theresa O'Connor

Context:
In this case, a medical center encounters tragedy, leaving its top executive wondering how confidence can ever be restored.

Theresa O'Connor is rushing to get to work. She is running late, delayed by a lengthy breakup with her now-former boyfriend of 10 months, Brian Rollins. Breakups are always difficult, so Theresa planned things as best as possible, meeting with him face-to-face to deliver the bad news, and ensuring that she had time to address Brian's questions and concerns. Theresa was interested in maintaining a friendship with Brian, but she had lost her romantic interest in him, as he was much too possessive, something that very much offended her because she was a fiercely independent person.

Theresa believed that the breakup session would go better rather than worse, but she was very wrong. Brian was crushed, begging her to change her mind and give the relationship another chance, and even shedding what appeared to be a tear or two. But Theresa's mind was made up. Realizing that nothing she could say would make things any better, she departed Brian's residence and made her way to work, albeit very late.

Theresa serves as a physical therapist for Eastover Medical Center and, being a fitness buff, she also works part-time as an aerobics instructor at Eastover Wellness, a comprehensive wellness center owned and operated by Eastover Medical Center. Eastover Wellness is physically attached to Eastover Medical Center, a 290-bed, for-profit provider of general medical and surgical services based in Pinehurst, a city with a population of 229,121, located in the Pacific region of the United States. Eastover Medical Center has a 50-year history in Pinehurst, with its wellness center being established just 2 years ago.

Theresa's full-time position as a physical therapist is based in the establishment's physical therapy and rehabilitative services division. Because this particular division extensively uses Eastover Wellness for various therapies, the wellness center was constructed in close proximity to the division, making it quick and easy for Theresa to walk over after the day's physical therapy work to teach her aerobics classes in the evenings. Eastover Wellness features state-of-the-art fitness equipment, including treadmills, stationary bicycles, elliptical machines, and more, along with an indoor swimming pool, racquetball court, and track. Theresa deeply enjoys both her physical therapy and aerobics instruction opportunities and she works very hard to serve her customers well.

Immediately on her arrival at Eastover Medical Center to begin the day's work, Theresa apologized to staff members for being late. Entering her workstation, the telephone calls from Brian began, with calls being directed to both her work and cellular telephone numbers. Brian initially was very sincere on the calls, but then initiated a very aggressive and mean tone, demanding that Theresa reconsider her decision to end their relationship. Theresa at first tried to handle the matter professionally by politely communicating with him, but her efforts were in vain and she was forced to simply forward the calls to her voice mailbox. She continued with the morning's work. On her lunch break, she was about to leave the building but noticed Brian in the parking lot, blocking her car in with his. Fortunately, she noticed this before leaving the building, called Eastover Medical Center's security, and had the security guards escort Brian off campus. Brian clearly was exhibiting signs of anger and distress and this struck fear in Theresa's heart.

The commotion at lunch was so pronounced that it got the attention of Rachel McIntyre, Director of Physical Therapy and Rehabilitative Services, who asked Theresa for details, after which she ensured that Eastover Medical Center's security was heightened. Being a good friend of Theresa's, in addition to a work colleague, Rachel invited Theresa to stay at her house over the coming days to decrease the chances that she would encounter Brian, who very much had become feared, given his increasingly erratic behavior. Over subsequent days, the telephone calls from Brian kept coming, but Theresa just ignored them, hoping for the best.

But things quickly seemed to be getting better. Surprisingly, about 10 days after giving Brian the bad news, Theresa received a handwritten letter in the mail from him indicating that he had made peace with the breakup. The telephone calls ceased and Theresa believed that her life would get back to normal, without the constant fear in the back of her mind that Brian would suddenly appear. Although she initially believed that she could be friends with Brian, his inappropriate handling of the breakup ruled that out completely. Relieved, Theresa moved on.

Seven days later, Theresa reported on a Thursday evening for her part-time job as an aerobics instructor at Eastover Wellness. She was very excited because this was the first time that she was scheduled to teach a water aerobics class. On her arrival, she greeted her students and after a brief introduction, the class of 20 took to the water in the wellness center's indoor swimming pool. About 15 minutes into the session, Theresa heard a loud bang at the front desk area of the wellness center, followed by the sounds of shattering glass. Brian suddenly appeared in the swimming pool area, dressed in black, carrying a cache of weapons, firing bullets at anyone and everyone. The sound of gunshots rung out across campus. Telephone calls to emergency services immediately were placed by anyone who was not in the line of fire. Eastover Medical Center's security department immediately responded, as did the Pinehurst Police Department. But by the time law enforcement arrived, the massacre was over. After killing seven people, including Theresa, and injuring ten others, Brian turned one of his guns on himself. The water aerobics students had literally been sitting ducks, unable to quickly take cover. The swimming pool was a sea of blood.

Officers from Pinehurst's Police Department, assisted by Eastover Medical Center's security guards, immediately locked down the entire medical center. The establishment's emergency management plan was enacted, with all senior managers and other critical parties reporting at once to the facility. The medical center was searched to ensure that other destructive persons or things were not on the premises. Casualties were addressed by the emergency department at the medical center. A short time later, officers discovered Brian's car in the parking lot and, on its front seat, the note he had left detailing his plans for the massacre, blaming Theresa for destroying his life. Law enforcement officers were all too familiar with this type of scenario, educated on such as a result of its periodic occurrence across the nation, where a spurned lover goes about seeking revenge in a most brutal way. Within an hour, the facility was declared to be secured.

Almost immediately, the massacre became a local and then national news story. Satellite trucks from news stations appeared seemingly instantaneously, with their reporters eager to get details. Susan Norton, Eastover Medical Center's President and Chief Executive Officer, provided a brief statement extending her condolences to the friends and families of the victims, as police and medical center personnel worked to identify victims and notify loved ones. This was the tragedy of tragedies.

Eastover Wellness was immediately closed until further notice. The 2-year-old establishment that served as a bastion of health and wellness, in the matter of an instant, became the symbol of death and destruction. Over coming days and weeks, funerals were held, media reports continued, internal and external investigations were conducted, and tears were shed. Susan, in meetings with her senior managers, wondered how the institution would ever recover. After such a massacre, she could not imagine how confidence could ever be restored.

DISCUSSION

1. In this case, Eastover Medical Center faced the tragedy of tragedies in that a domestic matter spilled over into the workplace and,
unfortunately, resulted in loss of life, not only for the primary target,
but also for a number of patrons of the medical center. Setting aside
the human tragedy of the event, what actions would be required
of the institution's marketing department in the days, weeks, and
months following the tragedy?

2. Despite the human loss resulting from the massacre, Eastover
Medical Center eventually will have to move on. What actions might
Eastover Medical Center take to restore the public's confidence in
the institution? What role would the establishment's marketing department play in this restoration?

3. The case indicated that, after the massacre, Eastover Wellness was
shut down indefinitely, but we have no indication of what eventually happened. How do you think Eastover Medical Center should
handle Eastover Wellness? Should it be reopened or not? What
options might be considered? Which option would you choose
and why?

4. Eastover Medical Center and Eastover Wellness were physically con-
nected, meaning that the tragedy could just as easily have occurred
in any area of the establishment. Given this, what sort of impact
would you anticipate the Eastover Wellness massacre to have on
the other services offered by Eastover Medical Center? How might
the institution work to separate Eastover Wellness from Eastover
Medical Center in the minds of consumers?

5. Both the medical center and its wellness component shared the
same brand name—Eastover. In technical terms, Eastover Wellness
is known as a brand extension, carrying an existing brand name
that, in this case, is that of its parent company. There are advantages
and disadvantages to this sort of thing. Using a standard marketing
textbook and other marketing resources, make a list of the advantages and disadvantages associated with using brand extensions,
as opposed to newly developed brand names for given products.
Having read this case, you already know of one disadvantage.

PART THREE

Marketing Management

CHAPTER 17

Battling Pies
in the Sky

SNAPSHOT

Institution:

Terrace Hospital, a 125-bed, not-for-profit rural hospital providing general medical and surgical services

Locations:

Lexington (population 14,682), a rural community located in the West South Central region of the United States

Fairmont (population 38,314), a very cosmopolitan, suburban community located 20 miles to the south of Lexington

Clearwater (population 196,520), an urban community located 35 miles to the south of Lexington

Characters:

Mr. Peter Brooks, Administrator

Ms. Katherine White, Director of Marketing

(both of Terrace Hospital)

Context:

In this case, the top marketing officer of a rural hospital questions the institution's administrator for his decision to target a population that clearly is outside of the scope of the hospital's stated mission.

Katherine White, Director of Marketing at Terrace Hospital, has a very big concern. She faithfully has served in her 125-bed, not-for-profit institution for over 7 years, working for Administrator Peter Brooks, whom she largely admires. But on occasion, Peter overlooks her professional advice as well as the advice of her fellow senior managers, sometimes not even requesting such before important decisions are made. Very often, negative consequences result and this, Katherine fears, is one of those occasions.

Katherine is professionally trained in marketing, having earned a Bachelor of Science in the discipline and a Master of Business Administration, and she heavily believes in following textbook guidance in making marketing decisions. Peter, however, tends to follow his instincts, often getting so excited about ideas that he decides to pursue them before proper analyses can be conducted to determine their viability. Peter's recklessness is not the result of malice or incompetence, but is derived from his overly optimistic mindset that must be tempered by his more balanced-thinking colleagues who are better at weighing the advantages and disadvantages of given pursuits.

Peter's "shoot from the hip" approach has almost always produced adverse consequences, but fortunately the damage historically has been minimal. Thanks to the damage control efforts of Peter's senior staff members, including Katherine, Terrace Hospital has never suffered any true hardships from his overeager tendencies. With his most recent pursuit, however, Peter is more headstrong than ever and the stakes are much higher, leading to Katherine's heightened concerns.

This all started 1 week ago when, bright and early on a Monday morning, Katherine was called into Peter's office where he excitedly communicated that he had come up with a sure thing for Terrace Hospital. He went on to state that the institution will be placing a clinic in a new market and needs Katherine to fast-track marketing communications materials for a grand opening that is less than 3 months away.

Katherine was not surprised by the short timeline. Terrace Hospital operated seven rural medical clinics in towns as small as 900 residents and every one of them seemed to be opened practically overnight on a shoestring budget. The hospital had great success in doing so, largely because the rural areas that were targeted had absolutely no competitors, but very needful populations who welcomed Terrace Hospital's clinics with open arms.

But this time, Peter deviated from Terrace Hospital's usual pursuits, opting for something entirely different. Instead of targeting the population of a rural community, he decided that the time was right to enter a very cosmopolitan marketplace, Fairmont, situated on the outskirts of the largest city in the state, Clearwater. Not only is Fairmont a cosmopolitan marketplace, it is considered to be the most competitive market in the region. Fairmont was as far removed from rural America as one could possibly imagine. On hearing this, Katherine was speechless.

Katherine knows that in urban and suburban environments, the cards are stacked against Terrace Hospital—and in a big way. The hospital is located in Lexington, a rural community of 14,682 situated in the West South Central region of the United States. The town is positioned on the outskirts of a burgeoning area, centered on Clearwater, a city of 196,520, and numerous suburbs, one of which is Fairmont (population 38,314). Of the suburbs surrounding Clearwater, Fairmont is the fastest growing and wealthiest, acting for the most part as a commuter city for Clearwater, offering prominent homes, shops, and other establishments, including a range of medical clinics, mostly affiliated with the large medical centers of Clearwater.

Peter believes that, given the fast growth of Fairmont, a patient base would be easy to establish. He also believes that the wealthy population in Fairmont could provide a satisfactory income stream for Terrace Hospital, first by clinic patronage in Fairmont and second by referrals of patients to Terrace Hospital in Lexington should clinic patients be in need of more extensive medical testing and treatment.

Katherine sees problems with Peter's views on multiple fronts. Among other things, the marketing budgets of the clinics in Fairmont and their associated medical centers in Clearwater are immense, dwarfing the entire operating budget of Terrace Hospital. Even with a strong move into the market, Terrace Hospital would never be able to withstand a prolonged marketing communications battle, as its funding would run dry, upon which it would be pummeled by competitors.

Another problem centers on consumer traffic patterns in Fairmont, which run almost exclusively from the municipality to areas in and around Clearwater. Lexington is literally and figuratively out of the transit loops connecting the nearby urban and suburban areas, being located approximately 35 miles away from Clearwater and 20 miles away from Fairmont just off an interstate highway.

As a rural outpost, Lexington is neither where the citizens of Fairmont work nor play. Hence, referrals from Terrace Hospital's proposed clinic in Fairmont to its hospital in Lexington would be unlikely due to massive customer inconvenience, taking patients into a geographic area that would be considered foreign to them. The same could not be said for the typical Fairmont clinic, which has ties with medical centers in Clearwater, making for a more familiar, accessible, and convenient option for medical care, in the event that referrals for more complex treatments are required.

Further, Terrace Hospital primarily serves a poorer demographic, far different from the clientele of the clinics currently located in Fairmont. Even if Terrace Hospital's proposed Fairmont clinic was geared toward a more upscale market and transportation concerns proved to not be problematic, referrals back to Lexington likely would be unsuccessful, given Terrace Hospital's reputation as a rural healthcare provider, primarily serving the underprivileged.

Perhaps worst of all in Katherine's eyes, pursuit of the cosmopolitan population of Fairmont clearly violates the current mission statement of Terrace Hospital, which specifically mentions that Terrace Hospital exists to serve the medical care needs of the rural community in and around Lexington. Clearly, the population of Fairmont does not fit the profile of Terrace Hospital's mission-specified target market.

As Katherine sees it, Terrace Hospital's proposed Fairmont clinic will face competitors who are superior in every respect, catering to an unfamiliar demographic that is counter to mission-stipulated populations, promoting a referral network that is inconveniently located for Fairmont's residents. Katherine's perspectives are not the result of marketing research—she has not had the time to formally evaluate Fairmont for possible expansion opportunities—but logic, resulting from her education and experience, suggests that Terrace Hospital has no business entering Fairmont.

Despite Katherine's best efforts to convince Peter otherwise, he remained certain that Terrace Hospital will be successful in Fairmont and directed her to develop marketing communications materials accordingly. It is now 1 week later and neither Katherine nor any of her fellow senior managers have been able to reason with Peter. As she looked upon a few figures collected by Peter for commercial leases for the proposed clinic in Fairmont, Katherine felt as though this time, Peter's whims might actually result in very real financial harm to Terrace Hospital. Something had to be done, but she was at a loss as to what.

DISCUSSION

1. In this case, Peter appears to make decisions without intensive thought and analysis and he likely has his senior managers to thank for his continued tenure at Terrace Hospital. In thinking over the myriad elements in this case, together with your knowledge of marketing, what approach should Peter have taken to address his idea of expanding into the Fairmont marketplace?

2. Katherine admits that she has not conducted formal marketing research on expansion opportunities in the Fairmont market. Instead, she based her preliminary opinions of Peter's expansion idea on logic coming from her formal education and years of marketing experience. Do you believe Katherine's assessment was on target? Why or why not?

3. As the case concludes, Katherine appears to be at a loss, not knowing what she should do to change Peter's mind. If you were in Katherine's position, what actions would you take and why? Does this situation warrant breaking the chain of command and contacting Terrace Hospital's governing board? Why or why not?

4. Assume that the governing board of Terrace Hospital steps in and prohibits Peter from pursuing his plan to open a clinic in Fairmont. What argument might Peter make to convince them otherwise?

5. Assume alternatively, that the governing board of Terrace Hospital sides with Peter and authorizes his plan to open a clinic in Fairmont. How might a small institution with seemingly everything going against it compete with the large, wealthy medical establishments of Fairmont and, by association, Clearwater?

18

Embracing Missions

SNAPSHOT

Institution:
Oakridge University Hospital, a 525-bed, public teaching hospital affiliated with Oakridge University

Location:
Hamilton (population 1,328,984), located in the East South Central region of the United States

Characters:
Mr. Bruce Faulkner, Assistant Manager of Central Supply
Ms. Sherry Graham, Respiratory Therapist
Ms. Elizabeth Murphy, Director of Nursing
(all of Oakridge University Hospital)

Context:
In this case, a top nursing executive in a public teaching hospital grows concerned when she encounters employees holding negative attitudes toward the establishment's underprivileged patient population.

Elizabeth Murphy, Director of Nursing at Oakridge University Hospital, cannot wait to get off of her feet for her lunch break. It has been a very busy morning, she is hungry, and she desperately is in need of a moment to catch her breath. On her way to the cafeteria, she navigates around and through several construction areas placed throughout the massive 525-bed public teaching hospital, located in Hamilton, a city of 1,328,984 situated in the East South Central region of the United States.

The minor inconveniences associated with the construction are relatively new to her and her fellow Oakridge University Hospital employees, resulting from the hospital's efforts to upgrade a number of patient waiting areas, repaint several main corridors, and make a number of other functional and aesthetic enhancements. Ultimately, through these upgrades, the establishment hopes to improve patient access and comfort at Oakridge University Hospital.

As she makes her way into the hospital's cafeteria and purchases her meal, Elizabeth spots two very familiar faces who invite her to join them for lunch. They are Sherry Graham, a Respiratory Therapist, and Bruce Faulkner, an Assistant Manager in the hospital's central supply department. Joining them at their table, she eagerly awaits the latest news—and the topic of the day pertained to the hospital's construction. While each of Elizabeth's two lunch mates were pleased with the construction, noting that it would make for a better working environment for staff members, their comments regarding the benefits to Oakridge University Hospital's patients were less sincere, something Elizabeth found to be very troubling.

Bruce questioned using hospital resources to improve patient waiting areas. He remarked that since the hospital is always full, why should money be spent to improve convenience and comfort for patients. He continued on, noting that the hospital certainly does not have to worry about customer traffic, especially as it is the healthcare provider of last resort for most patients who are too poor to go anywhere else. Sherry agreed with Bruce, adding that the hospital had no reason to fear competitors stealing Oakridge University Hospital's patient population. She expressed that because most of Oakridge University Hospital's patients, as Medicaid or charity cases, were not paying for their care anyway, they were not truly deserving of the enhancements being made by the new construction projects. Sherry simply could not understand the rationale for doing more for Oakridge University Hospital's patient population.

Elizabeth, a 30-year veteran of the hospital, was dumbfounded by the views expressed by Bruce and Sherry. Arguing that all patients should be treated with respect and dignity, she responded that one of the central reasons for Oakridge University Hospital's existence is to treat patients without sufficient financial resources and noted that this obligation is clearly expressed in its mission statement. As a mission mandate, Elizabeth conveyed that Oakridge University Hospital and its employees have an obligation to these patients, making them important and deserving of the best health care that can possibly be offered.

Elizabeth was particularly quick to correct Sherry regarding her belief that Oakridge University Hospital's patients are nonpayers. Sure, they may not have the means to open their wallets and pay for healthcare services, she expressed, but government programs provide funding on their behalf that the hospital would not receive otherwise. Technically, they are paying customers, the money just does not come from their pocketbooks.

Finishing up what turned out to be an unpleasant lunch experience, Elizabeth noted that even if Oakridge University Hospital never received a single penny from any source to pay for the healthcare costs of its clients, the patients of Oakridge University Hospital still deserve the best of care and attention. Finishing off her comments, she questioned the two, asking why they would even wish to work at Oakridge University Hospital if they did not see the value of both its mission and the rewards of serving the needy.

Returning to her office, Elizabeth reflected on her lunch experience. While she was concerned that both Bruce and Sherry embraced such views, she was particularly troubled that Sherry would do so, because she is involved in the direct delivery of care to patients. If she harbored feelings in her heart and mind that Oakridge University Hospital's patients did not deserve the comfort and convenience of enhanced patient waiting areas, how might this impact the quality of the care that she provided?

But what Elizabeth perhaps viewed to be most troubling did not pertain to Bruce or Sherry specifically, but instead dealt with the fact that she had heard time and time again the same thing from many of Oakridge University Hospital's employees. In prior years, she had even spoken with Oakridge University Hospital's top administrators about the matter, seeking guidance in how she should handle what at best is an uncaring attitude regarding patients, and at worst could lead to the inappropriate treatment of patients and even death. Sadly though, the top officials did not have much guidance to offer, noting public sector bureaucracy and complexities associated with disciplining employees, especially in cases where there are no tangible infractions. Elizabeth found this to be very frustrating.

While Elizabeth always tried to educate and enlighten employees holding negative beliefs about Oakridge University Hospital's patient population, she knew that her success at converting them was at best very limited. Thankfully, she did not view the mindset held by Bruce, Sherry, and others to be epidemic, but did view it to be prominent enough to warrant concern. And there was at least a degree of comfort in knowing that the problem was not limited to Oakridge University Hospital, as, through her network of professional contacts, she came to realize that the mindset was rather commonplace at public hospitals serving the underprivileged.

In trying to craft a theory on the origins of such a negative and unproductive mindset, Elizabeth's best guess was that it simply was an artifact of the institution's culture and characteristics. She well knew that Oakridge University Hospital did not possess a marketing culture; that its employees did not view themselves to be customer service agents or ambassadors on behalf of the institution. And she well knew that a constant and unending flow of patients who possessed few if any other options for medical care certainly could instill a mindset of complacency in employees and the institutions in which they served. Further, she knew that the size of Oakridge University Hospital did not help matters, as the employee base was so large that massive bureaucracy was a given, making even seasoned employees feel more like a number than an individual person. Elizabeth reasoned that all of this and more set the stage for negative mindsets at Oakridge University Hospital.

Regardless, Elizabeth could not understand why employees would care to work for an institution that embraced a mission that they personally deemed to be unacceptable. She wondered why they would not desire working elsewhere; somewhere that supported a mission they personally viewed to be acceptable. Their motives defied comprehension.

Elizabeth cared very much for Oakridge University Hospital's patients and, given her longtime experience at the hospital, she was committed to improvement on every front. Hearing Bruce and Sherry's perspectives brought back countless memories of other employees expressing similar views. She wondered what more she could do to improve the customer service and marketing orientations of Oakridge University Hospital's employees.

DISCUSSION

1. This case presents a very negative mindset harbored by at least some employees at Oakridge University Hospital. What are the possible ramifications for patients at Oakridge University Hospital or any other facility who encounter employees possessing the mindset held by Bruce and Sherry? Do you believe that such a negative employee mindset can result in tangible patient harm, or is the mindset simply a personal expression that would not be extended to the care and treatment of patients? Please justify your responses.

2. Assume that you are Sherry's supervisor and you receive a telephone call from Elizabeth who conveys the perspectives that were echoed by Sherry over lunch. Would you bring the matter up with Sherry? Why or why not? If you did indeed address Sherry, what approach would you take and what would you expect to gain by your actions?

3. Elizabeth attributes the negative perspectives of the patient population held by Bruce, Sherry, and some others at Oakridge University Hospital to be the product of culture, a burgeoning supply of patients with few alternatives, and bureaucracy. Assuming that she is correct, how might you go about stemming negative sentiment?

4. Elizabeth noted that she had approached the top executives at Oakridge University Hospital and asked for guidance as to how she should address employees when hearing negative perspectives regarding the hospital's patient base. Much to her dismay, she did not receive any particularly beneficial advice. What does this say about the executives she consulted?

5. This case presents an account by a nursing executive who encountered a negative mindset held by at least some of Oakridge University Hospital's employees. Suppose that Elizabeth had been accompanied by a marketing manager during her lunch meeting with Bruce and Sherry. Would you anticipate the marketing manager's perspectives on the matter to be similar to Elizabeth's, less intense, or more intense? Please justify your response.

CHAPTER 19

Enough Is Enough

SNAPSHOT

Institution:
Brighton Court, a 60-unit, for-profit provider of luxury assisted-living services

Location:
Princeton (population 42,567), located in the South Atlantic region of the United States

Characters:
Mr. Richard Cooper, Owner and Administrator
Ms. Elizabeth Hall, Resident
(both of Brighton Court)

Context:
In this case, the owner and administrator of a provider of luxury assisted-living services must make a difficult decision when faced with an unruly resident.

Richard Cooper is facing a major dilemma. For the past 7 years, Brighton Court, a luxury assisted-living center, has been providing exemplary service to the individuals occupying its 60 residential units, but now the establishment is facing accusations of inferior service by none other than one of its own residents, with her family members even becoming involved.

Brighton Court has a policy of delivering excellent customer service to all patrons of the establishment and Richard, along with every staff member at the property, takes this to heart, working feverishly to attend to the wants and needs of residents.

But all of this service and attention apparently is not enough to satisfy Elizabeth Hall, a 76-year-old widow who moved to Brighton Court 4 months ago, shortly after the death of her husband. Following the usual protocol, Richard and his staff members met with Elizabeth and her family members, touring them around the property and arranging proper evaluations to ensure that Brighton Court could properly accommodate Elizabeth as a resident. In the end, Elizabeth entered Brighton Court as a resident in what was anticipated to be a productive relationship, but given the complaint behavior exhibited by Elizabeth both at the onset of her residency and continuing on to present day, the relationship has been anything but productive.

Brighton Court is located in Princeton, a city of 42,567 situated in the South Atlantic region of the United States. The property is ideally positioned, offering easy access via automobile and air transportation in a climate considered to be ideal almost year round. As a smaller property, Brighton Court is very quaint, permitting occupants to know each and every other resident. Patterned after a resort hotel, the establishment offered the usual array of luxury accommodations, including 24-hour security, room service, indoor and outdoor swimming pools, tennis courts, a state-of-the-art fitness center, and a 9-hole golf course. Coastal views and lush gardens provide yet another exclusive touch on what unsurprisingly happens to be a very expensive accommodation.

The assisted-living center was the brainchild of Richard who, after gaining a decade of experience in long-term care establishments, decided to establish his own assisted-living center, making his vision a reality by providing a special combination of luxury and security to the senior population. The center consistently has received top marks by its residents and also by editors of senior living guides, yielding a constant stream of inquiries regarding vacancies and a never-ending waiting list. The resulting and highly positive word-of-mouth acted to communicate the benefits of Brighton Court to others, reducing the need to direct resources to advertising and other forms of marketing communication. Richard is very proud of Brighton Court's marketplace performance as the results serve as an indicator of a job well done.

But now all of the hard work invested by Richard and his staff members is in jeopardy because, for the first time ever, Brighton Court is experiencing a resident who simply cannot be satisfied, regardless of the effort and attention delivered. Literally, from her first day at the property, Elizabeth has complained. First, it was her residential unit's climate control system, with Elizabeth complaining that the temperature in her room was never comfortable. After numerous tests by maintenance department personnel, nothing was found to be out of order or functioning improperly. Even a handheld thermometer placed in Elizabeth's residential unit confirmed the accuracy of the climate control system. This, however, was insufficient in Elizabeth's eyes, ending with her grumbling that she would simply have to deal with a faulty system being in her residential unit. Staff members even offered to transfer her to another unit to ensure her satisfaction. She refused to move.

One month later, Elizabeth forwarded another complaint, this one being that the food provided by Brighton Court was inedible. This was a shock to the staff members of Brighton Court, as the establishment's food quality was exactly the same as that offered by restaurants in luxury hotels. Regardless, Elizabeth rejected any attempt by staff members to provide meals, demanding that her children deliver meals to her on a daily basis. This hardship brought Elizabeth's children into the fray, with both of them, in turn, demanding that Brighton Court better address her meal concerns.

With Elizabeth filing two major complaints in her first 2 months at Brighton Court, Richard invited Elizabeth's children to have lunch with him at the establishment with the goal of discussing Brighton Court's efforts to address her complaints. During lunch, he addressed the prior issue involving Elizabeth's complaint regarding the climate control system in her residential unit and the steps that had been taken to ensure her satisfaction, stating that it appeared that she now was satisfied with their efforts—or at least she had made up her mind to simply tolerate matters. Regardless, that particular issue seemed to have disappeared.

Noticing that each of Elizabeth's two children had cleaned their entire lunch plates, he also informed them that their meal was one of three lunch options that was served to residents of Brighton Court on that given day. He ensured them that the food was of very high quality and that perhaps Elizabeth might be overly critical, both of the food and the efforts made to address her issues. The children apologized on Elizabeth's behalf and noted that she had the tendency to be a bit stubborn and selfish, making gigantic issues out of simple problems; something they noticed to be on the increase following her husband's death. After paying Elizabeth a visit, they thanked Richard for his efforts and departed.

Shortly thereafter, Elizabeth began eating Brighton Court meals and seemed to be over her complaint behavior, with Richard and his staff members breathing a sigh of relief that perhaps she had begun to adjust to her new life in assisted-living accommodations. Their relief did not last long.

During her third month at Brighton Court, Elizabeth filed yet another complaint, this one because, in her view, attendants did not report in a timely fashion when she summoned them to her residential unit with her call button. Further, she was telephoning residents in other units to complain about what she termed to be shoddy service and overall poor quality. Fortunately, her gripes did not carry any weight with her peers, but they did result in Richard receiving call after call from valued residents, notifying him that Elizabeth was harassing them with her constant complaining. They further communicated that Elizabeth was upsetting the peaceful, collegial, and cooperative atmosphere that led them to select Brighton Court for assisted-living services. The residents demanded that Richard take action to restore serenity at the establishment.

Working toward resolving what had now become a crisis, Richard called a meeting with several of his key staff members to decide on a proper course of action. On one hand, Brighton Court personnel communicated that they wanted to serve Elizabeth, but on the other, they were beginning to realize that their efforts were in vain, because she did not appear to be capable of being satisfied regardless of the devoted time, attention, and resolution. Aside from her formal complaints, staff members were constantly being summoned to her unit for even the smallest of requests, almost all of them being beyond their service duties and responsibilities.

Further discussion brought about resolution. Staff members were in agreement that while they valued the opportunity to serve Elizabeth, she crossed the line when she began agitating other residents. Given this, they believed that they could no longer continue to offer her a home at Brighton Court, especially when residential units were in high demand from others who would likely be appreciative of the high level of service provided by the establishment. Perhaps of greatest concern to staff members, Elizabeth's complaint behaviors might escalate, potentially reaching the larger community, harming Brighton Court's hard-earned, pristine image. That was more than enough for Richard. Believing that Brighton Court could make a strong case for her eviction, he picked up the telephone to arrange an immediate meeting with Elizabeth's children.

DISCUSSION

1. Elizabeth appeared to be unreceptive to Brighton Court's efforts to accommodate her, even after multiple attempts to do so were forwarded by the assisted-living center. While the case does not provide enough information to ascertain the reasons for her complaint behavior or all of the potential underlying causes for such, in your opinion, are there customers who simply are unable to be satisfied? Please justify your response and also communicate your solutions for handling these difficult customers.

2. While the case does not indicate the ultimate outcome, it does appear that Brighton Court is moving toward evicting Elizabeth. Do you believe Brighton Court is justified in evicting her from the property? Why do you believe this to be the case?

3. Assume that Elizabeth's children plead with Richard to give her another chance and he does so. What actions could Brighton Court take to ensure a peaceful living environment for the residents of the assisted-living center?

4. While this case might, on the surface, not appear to be related to marketing, it actually is in that there are many marketing ramifications. Richard and his staff members were aware of this as they had concerns that Elizabeth's complaints might reach the greater community and damage Brighton Court's reputation. Assume the worst, that Elizabeth is granted a reprieve and permitted to remain a resident, but then contacts the media and government agencies claiming abuse at Brighton Court. Setting legal actions aside, if you were Richard, how would you handle this from a public relations perspective?

5. Richard noted that a lengthy waiting list and excellent word-of-mouth publicity permitted Brighton Court to forgo the use of advertising and other forms of marketing communication to promote the establishment. Although there might be justifications for limiting marketing communications, the need for marketing remains. To demonstrate your knowledge of this, refer to a comprehensive definition of marketing in a basic marketing textbook and, with Brighton Court as the entity of focus, discuss the aspects of marketing that Richard must address outside of marketing communications.

20

All the Wrong Moves

SNAPSHOT

Institution:
York Clinic, a single-physician medical practice specializing in family medicine

Location:
Concord (population 594,210), located in the West North Central region of the United States

Characters:
Ms. Christy Summers, Administrator
Dr. Robert York, Owner and Physician
(both of York Clinic)

Context:
In this case, a recently hired clinic administrator works toward resolving patient overcrowding but discovers that her remedy is very different than that of the clinic's physician owner.

Christy Summers, Administrator of York Clinic, is very concerned. She has only recently joined the clinic, working for its owner, Dr. Robert York, but 6 months into her new job, she is shocked by what she views to be inefficient and ineffective operations, culminating to create poor patient experiences. Thankfully, quality of care is not at issue, but quality of the patient experience, including patient comfort and convenience, is suffering dramatically, prompting Christy's concerns. With 6 months under her belt, Christy believes that it is now time to confront Dr. York with her growing concerns.

Dr. York founded York Clinic 30 years ago, immediately setting up the practice following his medical training. The clinic is located in Concord, a city of 594,210 located in the West North Central region of the United States. While there are many competing clinics and health services establishments in Concord, Dr. York has carved out a very loyal and ever-growing following of patients.

As for Christy, she is a very experienced clinic manager, having served in various management capacities for over 15 years. Through her years of service in healthcare institutions, she came to know Dr. York, who forwarded an employment offer to her 8 months ago. She initially was reluctant to join the clinic because it was a very small operation, far different from her employment as an ambulatory care manager at a local hospital, but on further discussions with Dr. York, she believed the challenges and opportunities would be great enough to justify her move to York Clinic.

Coming in with high expectations, Christy's new opportunity got off to a quick start. Acclimating herself to clinic operations, Christy was astonished at York Clinic's patient volume—all for a single practitioner. The volume was, in fact, too brisk for the clinic's capacity, causing massive bottlenecks in service delivery. By her estimation, after monitoring patient waits extending beyond designated appointment times, the average delay was in the neighborhood of 50 minutes. Scheduled appointments were enough to cause bottlenecks alone—patients were double booked at given appointment times—but this was further exacerbated by York Clinic's policy of welcoming walk-in patients.

All in all, the glut of patients brought operations to a crawl. As a result, the clinic's personnel were forced to serve primarily as traffic control officers and secondarily as clinical and administrative staff members. Dr. York also was forced to see patients only for the briefest of time periods, creating dissension among some of his patients who desired more "face time" with their physician. Given the burden on the employees of York Clinic, Christy was very concerned that errors in treatment might occur, potentially putting patients' lives at risk. Administrative errors were also a very real possibility.

Christy viewed excessive patient traffic to have further ramifications; namely involving patient comfort and convenience. The clinic's waiting room was bursting at the seams and its parking lot was overflowing with patient vehicles. Christy knew that this simply could not continue. Clinic operations would be much more efficient and effective if employees, including Dr. York, had personal and professional space, permitting them to concentrate on their given duties and responsibilities without having a crowd-control mindset. And patient satisfaction, something that according to recent surveys could stand to be shored up, likely would improve.

Christy also has come to realize that the situation is not about to get any better. Dr. York has indicated that he is desirous of increased growth, even stating that he would like her to develop a marketing communications campaign designed to increase patient traffic. She can no longer remain passive on the matter.

Armed with facts and figures, Christy arranged a meeting with Dr. York. During this meeting, Christy carefully outlined her concerns, presenting relevant information regarding employee burdens, patient waiting times, inefficiencies resulting from bottlenecks, and so on, indicating that these encumbrances were diminishing the patient experience. Dr. York responded that he was aware of the problem and had already devised a solution—he planned to increase the size of the clinic's waiting room and parking lot.

Christy was not at all impressed. Dr. York's solution would only serve to place a bandage on a very complex problem, resolving very little. Sure, a larger waiting room and parking area would reduce overcrowding and help improve patient comfort and convenience, but these things would leave unresolved the issue of being more respectful of patients' time. An enlarged waiting room and parking lot simply would not diminish the nearly 1-hour delay past designated appointment times that was routinely experienced by patients. And these steps likely would only marginally improve patient satisfaction.

Christy went on to state that the real issue for resolution pertained not to insufficient waiting room or parking lot capacities, but instead involved insufficient practitioner capacity. In her view, York Clinic needed to hire another physician or possibly a physician assistant or nurse practitioner. Presenting her solution to Dr. York, she expressed that with increased practitioner capacity, the waiting room and parking lot expansions might not be needed as improved patient flow would eliminate bottlenecks.

But Dr. York was not keen on her proposed solution. He viewed the prospect of adding another clinician to simply be too expensive. He privately communicated to Christy that he had many things that he wanted in life and that in order to get these things he needed income. He was willing to work harder to see more patients and was willing to improve the physical setting of the clinic by increasing the size of the waiting room and parking area; however, additional caregivers would not be considered. He commented that patient loyalty would keep his patients returning, regardless of the obvious delays, diminishing the necessity, in his opinion, to increase practitioner capacity.

Christy was very disappointed by Dr. York's response. He seemed to have no conception that an increase in practitioner capacity, if executed properly, would actually place more money in his pocket, permitting him to reach his personal financial goals faster. And most importantly, the patient experience dramatically would be improved.

At this point, Christy wondered whether Dr. York's resistance to increasing practitioner capacity was the result of ignorance or simple greed. She perhaps was most offended by his lack of motivation to enhance the patient experience, viewing this to be unnecessary due to burgeoning patient traffic and high patient loyalty. Christy never took patient patronage for granted, striving to seek constant improvements, whether they were or were not demanded by patients. This, in her view, was the proper way to serve patients, maintain loyalty, and defend against competition.

Just 6 months into her employment at York Clinic, Christy is beginning to have doubts as to whether she made the right decision to join the medical practice. Given vast differences between her philosophy and that of Dr. York, she thinks it just may be time for her to move to another opportunity.

DISCUSSION

1. The respective solutions to the overcrowding problem at York Clinic offered by Christy and Dr. York are very different. What are your thoughts on these two very different approaches to the given issues experienced at the practice?
2. Aside from the options to address overcrowding at York Clinic, as expressed by Christy and Dr. York, there are other methods to reduce the bottlenecking experienced by patients at the practice. Based on the information supplied in the case, brainstorm on other possibilities and identify these options. Between Christy's idea, Dr. York's idea, and the options you formulated, which would you choose and why?

3. Christy indicated that she was offended by Dr. York's perspective that, despite clear inadequacies in practitioner availability and the resulting lack of timeliness in care delivery, there was no reason to enhance the patient experience due to burgeoning patient traffic and associated loyalty. What are your thoughts on Dr. York's mindset? What would you anticipate to be the ultimate impact of such a mindset on the operations of healthcare entities?

4. Patients at York Clinic experience significant delays past their scheduled appointment times before being seen by Dr. York. Unfortunately, such delays, regardless of their cause, are not terribly uncommon for patients. In some cases, such as overburdened emergency departments, delays are the result of uncontrollable circumstances. But in other situations, the delays are the result of improper planning, uncaring attitudes, and general disrespect for patients. Conduct a brief investigation to ascertain the particular techniques and incentives that other service industries use to ensure timely service delivery. How might these techniques be applied in the healthcare industry to improve service delivery?

5. The case of York Clinic draws attention to the importance of the patient experience, with Christy believing that the given experience at the clinic left much to be desired. What would you consider to be the ideal patient experience? Be sure to provide specific details.

CHAPTER 21

Just Blame Marketing

SNAPSHOT

Institution:
Eagle Ridge Optometry, a two-optometrist practice providing a range of optometry services

Location:
Fremont (population 34,674), located in the Mountain region of the United States

Characters:
Ms. Allison Bradford, Marketing Coordinator
Dr. Wayne Lucas, Co-Owner and Optometrist
Dr. Sheila Moore, Co-Owner and Optometrist
Mr. Ted Sullivan, Office Manager
(all of Eagle Ridge Optometry)

Context:
In this case, the marketing coordinator for an optometry practice is criticized for the poor performance of the establishment.

Allison Bradford, Marketing Coordinator for Eagle Ridge Optometry, is about to take up arms. The practice's patient traffic has not improved since she was hired 1 year ago. In fact, volume is down. This is worrisome enough for Allison, but to make matters worse, she is being blamed for the poor results and this has placed her employment in jeopardy. Allison knows that her efforts are not the cause of the practice's inferior performance and, fully in defensive mode, she plans to take a stand to protect herself and her reputation.

Eagle Ridge Optometry, an optometry practice based in Fremont (population 34,674) situated in the Mountain region of the United States, is owned by two optometrists, Drs. Wayne Lucas and Sheila Moore. The practice was established 14 years ago and has witnessed quite a bit of success over its history. More recently, however, patient volume has waned, primarily resulting from an increasing number of competitors in the city. Further, the rise of online options for purchasing eyeglasses and contact lenses has diminished opportunities for revenue, as has the increasing availability of laser vision correction services performed by ophthalmologists, with one such practice being based in Fremont. Eagle Ridge Optometry has found itself in a quandary, struggling to find a way to reinvigorate once-healthy levels of patient volume.

In seeking to revitalize growth, Drs. Lucas and Moore, together with Eagle Ridge Optometry's Office Manager, Ted Sullivan, believed that the practice should become more heavily involved in marketing in order to attract attention and generate patronage. Previously, the practice had only mildly been involved in marketing efforts, with Ted occasionally running advertisements in the local newspapers and on a few area radio stations. Conducted on a periodic basis, these efforts were somewhat unnecessary, because at the time, the practice faced little competition in the community. Customers generally had one of three choices for their eye care; otherwise, they would need to travel to another community to receive services. Hence, the market generally was captive, with outshopping posing little to no threat.

Economic development occurring in recent years brought new residents and an increasing number of businesses seeking to serve the wants and needs of Fremont's growing population. The number of eye care providers increased as well, with the city's first national optometry franchise opening 3 years ago, and its first ophthalmologist setting up a practice 2 years ago. Together with existing competitors, this put a strain on each practice in their efforts to secure and maintain a viable population of patients, as supply began to outstrip demand. Practices were forced to fight for patients, with many looking to advertising to do just that.

Drs. Lucas and Moore had hoped to avoid engagement in extensive advertising campaigns and other forms of marketing communication, but stagnation and retrenchment were occurring, forcing them to move vigorously into the area. As Ted already was heavily burdened with practice management duties, the decision was made to hire a marketing coordinator who could devote full-time efforts to building the practice. Allison was hired for the job.

Allison is relatively new to marketing, having earned a Bachelor of Business Administration with a major in Marketing from a New England university just prior to accepting the Eagle Ridge Optometry opportunity approximately 1 year ago. Despite her lack of practical experience, Allison is very well educated and has some sales experience from summer jobs held over the course of her university studies. She is very intelligent, never missing a place on the chancellor's list following each semester of work and she plans to translate her academic success into executive success.

Newly hired, Allison engaged in a 2-week orientation period, after which she went about devising the practice's first-ever marketing plan. Allison was given a modest, but seemingly adequate marketing communications budget, and formulated the marketing communications mix to the best of her ability. She called on advertising, namely, radio, newspaper, and billboard advertisements; public relations, namely, press releases announcing news that she deemed to be beneficial to the community; sales promotion, namely, free gifts distributed to patients and other publics of the practice; personal selling, namely, periodic visits made by herself to area establishments to discuss the practice's services; and direct marketing, namely, direct mail pieces posted to target audiences. Although she called on all five of the components of the traditional marketing communications mix, she did so in a modest fashion, spreading her budget across the various communicative mechanisms to maximize engagement with target audiences.

Allison was very proud of her work, but as the months rolled by she noticed a number of things that were very unsettling. Her most prominent concern pertained to the general sense of disrespect that was shown to patients by Eagle Ridge Optometry's employees. Admissions personnel were unenthusiastic, often addressing patients in a brash and demeaning fashion and occasionally even talking on their personal cellular telephones as they handled patient issues. Patient backlogs were very common, indicating inefficiencies running from the admissions desk through to patient examinations and discharge, with no one, not even the practice's optometrist owners, being concerned about such. This, in Allison's view, demonstrated tremendous disrespect for patients. Among all employees, the tone was casual, with them caring more about themselves than patients. Allison's eyes began to open wide, realizing that the practice's stagnation problem likely stemmed from an inferior product that perhaps sold well to the captive audiences of years past, but has since tanked, thanks to new, more respectful competitors who entered the market and permitted greater choice to the population of Fremont. Allison believed that Eagle Ridge Optometry probably had always conducted business in the current fashion, but now the consequences finally were being revealed very openly by patient flight.

Allison's greatest shock, however, came when she learned through the grapevine that her fellow employees were blaming her for the declining patient volume, with some claiming that her marketing communications efforts were off the mark. A few even accused her efforts of harming the business of the practice. This was most unsettling as Allison knew that her efforts were sound. The problem pertained to the poor level of service provided by everyone in the practice, from the lowest level employee all the way up to its two owners. Of course, Allison knew that she had to stay calm, because voicing her true opinions would likely lead to her termination, but she believed that may be coming anyway, as it appeared that the practice's employees were ganging up on her.

Knowing that if she permitted the discussion to continue behind her back, her fate definitely would be sealed, Allison decided to bring the matter out into the open by arranging a meeting with Ted, along with Drs. Lucas and Moore. In this meeting, Allison politely provided her observations, commenting on the grapevine allegations and providing a defense of her efforts. She noted that there were indications that her marketing communications activities were working, but their success was being sabotaged by the inferior provision of service to patients. Further, she offered her theory that the practice's poor performance in recent years likely had been a long time coming, and was only revealed as a result of new competitors which provided previously captive audiences an opportunity to escape to better service experiences.

The 22-year-old indeed had spoken. The room was completely silent. Drs. Lucas and Moore asked her to step out of the office while they conferred on the matter. Allison made her stand; now she awaits her fate.

DISCUSSION

1. Allison worked very hard to deliver marketing value on behalf of Eagle Ridge Optometry, yet she found that marketing communications excellence cannot mask an inferior product. Discuss the importance of ensuring that both product quality and communications quality are appropriately addressed in order to achieve success in the marketplace.

2. As the case concludes, it is obvious that Allison is becoming increasingly frustrated, especially on learning that her colleagues were seeking to blame her for the poor results of the practice. She decided to address the matter proactively by scheduling a meeting with Ted and the practice owners, giving her observations and defenses. Do you think this was an appropriate course of action? Why or why not? How might her approach have been improved?

3. What are your thoughts on Allison's theory that Eagle Ridge Optometry likely had always conducted business in the current fashion, but that problems only recently were revealed as a result of increased patient choice, courtesy of new competitors? Does her theory have merit? Please be sure to provide your rationale.

4. Reverse the situation presented in this case, placing product quality very high and marketing communications quality very low. Is this situation better than the reverse? Why or why not? If you were forced to choose between two business scenarios, one with high product quality and low marketing communications quality and the other with low product quality and high marketing communications quality, which would you choose and why?

5. Although the case provides no indication, based on the information provided, do you believe that Allison was fired? Why or why not?

PART FOUR

Marketing Strategy and Planning

The Elusive Marketing Culture

SNAPSHOT

Institution:

Victoria Medical Center, a 515-bed, not-for-profit hospital providing general medical and surgical services

Location:

Lincoln (population 277,251), located in the Pacific region of the United States

Characters:

Ms. Rebecca Lott, Vice President of Marketing
Mr. Louis Wright, President and Chief Executive Officer
(both of Victoria Medical Center)

Context:

In this case, the newly hired top marketing officer of a medical center turns to a unique method to determine whether the establishment possesses a marketing culture.

Rebecca Lott, the newly hired Vice President of Marketing at Victoria Medical Center, is about to conduct a simple field study on her first day of work. Specifically, she is going to walk through the facility and observe employees and their interactions with customers as a means of determining whether a marketing culture exists at Victoria Medical Center.

Her plan was devised 1 month ago, just after being hired, in a meeting with Louis Wright, Victoria Medical Center's President and Chief Executive Officer. Louis felt as though the medical center's employees were not focused enough on delivering high-quality customer service. He had been reading about the benefits of a marketing orientation and associated marketing culture and hoped that Rebecca could assist Victoria Medical Center in instituting this particular mindset and philosophy in the establishment.

Rebecca's field study could not have occurred at a better time. On her first day of work, almost no one will know her, cloaking her identity as a Victoria Medical Center executive. This will allow her the opportunity to move about the facility and monitor employee interactions with customers surreptitiously, permitting her to witness employee actions true to form, uninfluenced by the presence of a medical center authority.

This type of activity is one of Rebecca's favorites. In prior employment positions, she used mystery shoppers to better understand customer experiences and to serve as a device to keep employees on their toes, because they were all informed that mystery shopping was randomly used to assess business practices and processes. In this field experience, Rebecca, in essence, will be serving as a mystery shopper.

Victoria Medical Center could indeed use a marketing culture. As a not-for-profit medical center with 515 beds, the establishment is simply too large for direct managerial oversight of employees in all situations, particularly as they make their way in and around Victoria Medical Center's sprawling campus, encountering patients, their family members, and the numerous publics of the institution. As an urban medical center, situated in Lincoln, a city of 277,251 residents in the Pacific region of the United States, Rebecca knows that hospitality is a rare commodity in such environments, as employees often bring their big-city personas with them to work. But she has instituted marketing cultures in similar facilities in the past and knows that she can do the same at Victoria Medical Center.

Rebecca well understands that for the best organizational results to occur, every employee, regardless of job title or department, must act as an ambassador for Victoria Medical Center, ideally when both on and off campus. She views ambassadorial behaviors to be visible symbols of the existence of a marketing culture in the hearts and minds of employees. A good example of an ambassadorial behavior would be an employee's provision of assistance to customers, whether resulting from direct requests for such or in cases where they simply appear to be in need of assistance. Ambassadors improvise by thinking of customer wants and needs even before the customers themselves do, reaching out to assist on any and all occasions.

Another example of an ambassadorial behavior would be an employee's efforts to collect and dispose of trash and other refuse encountered as they go about their assigned duties and responsibilities. A staff member who, for example, is on his or her way to the cafeteria for a lunch break and happens to see an empty soft drink bottle left unattended on a waiting room table would provide great assistance to Victoria Medical Center by simply placing the bottle in a trash receptacle, helping to keep the campus beautiful. Such ambassadorial efforts are beneficial in both form and function, providing examples of excellent customer service witnessed by everyone at the medical center, as well as practical benefits resulting from the provided assistance.

As Rebecca arrived bright and early on her first day of work for a day of observation, she immediately noticed signs not of a marketing culture, but one of self-service from the perspectives of the vast majority of employees. Most employees were both not paying attention to their surroundings and bypassed opportunities to be of service to customers or overtly ignored needful customers altogether.

She observed one gentleman, pushing an elderly lady in a wheelchair, looking back and forth over and over again, apparently unable to find his way to an area of the medical center. Rebecca counted over 20 employees who walked past the pair without offering assistance, until one staff member finally stopped and directed the customers appropriately.

Examples of this happened continuously, with Rebecca herself interrupting her observation activities to intervene on occasion as she could not bear to see customers left unassisted. Opportunities to pitch in with litter control were universally ignored by every single employee she encountered. Rebecca even staged a simple experiment by dropping a paper towel on the floor of a main corridor. Despite it fluttering about as staff members walked past, no one made the effort to retrieve and dispose of the litter.

In Rebecca's final test, she posed as a lost patient herself, wandering around, looking back and forth, then down at a note in her hand to mimic an appointment slip, then up and down a hallway, creating the perfect illustration of a lost patient in need of direction. Dozens of employees simply walked past, inattentive and uncaring, until finally one stopped to offer assistance.

With her experiences recorded, Rebecca, based on the totality of her observations, gave Victoria Medical Center the grade of "D," viewing the presence of a marketing culture to be almost nonexistent. Later that day, she shared her experiences with Louis, who was not at all surprised by her findings.

Concerned about the prospects of improving employees' attentiveness to customers, Louis asked Rebecca if the establishment of a marketing culture was even possible, given that culture is very change resistant. Rebecca assured him that even in hardened organizations, instituting a marketing culture indeed is possible, as long as the commitment for such exists in executive ranks.

With top-level support, a proper plan can be formulated and implemented, yielding excellent results. Among other things, this plan will require studying the organization and devising appropriate structures (e.g., mission, vision, values, goals and objectives, educational opportunities, rewards, and so on) that facilitate the proliferation of ambassadorial mindsets and behaviors on the part of employees. She was confident that a marketing culture could be established at Victoria Medical Center.

After further discussions, Rebecca requested permission to arrange a few focus groups of both Victoria Medical Center's employees and customers to better understand the existing culture, upon which she could then formulate a structural plan for instituting a marketing culture. Louis liked the idea, offered her access to any needed resources, and asked her to keep him advised of her progress. Excited about the challenges ahead, Rebecca strolled to her office to begin her work.

DISCUSSION

1. Rebecca indicated that she enjoyed using the mystery shopping research technique to gain insights into customer experiences. Select a healthcare entity of your choice and formulate methods to use mystery shopping to learn about patient experiences. Present a detailed plan illustrating how you would go about implementing this technique in your selected healthcare establishment.

2. As a result of its many benefits, a marketing culture is highly desired by all healthcare organizations, yet its establishment in institutions seems to be very elusive. Why do you believe this to be the case?

3. Rebecca mentioned that a marketing culture requires structural elements designed in a manner to permit a marketing culture to flourish. Based on your knowledge of marketing and healthcare organizations, provide a detailed list of structural elements that would be helpful in the establishment of a marketing culture. Be sure to also explain why each of these elements would be beneficial in formulating such a culture.

4. Rebecca noted that marketing cultures seem to be especially foreign in urban healthcare institutions, as opposed, we assume, to suburban and rural establishments. Do you view hospitality, helpfulness, and other ambassadorial behaviors to be less prevalent in urban institutional environments than in their suburban and rural counterparts? Why or why not? Cite some examples of behaviors that you have witnessed.

5. Visit an area healthcare establishment for the purpose of determining the degree to which the institution possesses a marketing culture. Walk through the public areas of the facility and look for signs of hospitality, helpfulness, and other ambassadorial behaviors that are indicative of a marketing culture. After your experience, prepare a narrative describing what you witnessed and assign the institution a grade (i.e., A, B, C, D, or F) based on the quality of the particular marketing culture witnessed.

23

Words and Actions

SNAPSHOT

Institutions:
Clarksdale Medical Supplies, a retail distributor of durable medical equipment
Medical Star, a manufacturer of personal mobility products that are distributed through authorized resellers nationally
Castlewood Discount Drugs, a retail pharmacy that sells durable medical equipment, among many other items

Location:
Clarksdale (population 72,959), located in the West North Central region of the United States

Characters:
Mr. Benjamin Harvey
Ms. Rita Harvey
(both customers of Clarksdale Medical Supplies and Castlewood Discount Drugs)
Mr. Troy Irving, Owner, Clarksdale Medical Supplies
Mr. Randall Turner, Owner, Castlewood Discount Drugs

Context:
In this case, customers of a durable medical equipment retailer discover that the actual service experience does not measure up to the promises made in the store's advertisements.

Rita Harvey has learned her lesson. After years of witnessing advertisements touting the excellent service and support provided by Clarksdale Medical Supplies, a local durable medical equipment retailer, she decided to extend her patronage, purchasing a highly regarded wheelchair for her elderly husband. The initial experience was very pleasant, but on having difficulties with the item, Rita learned that the particular store's advertisements boasting of 100% satisfaction, money-back guarantees, and so forth were nothing more than empty words, not carrying any tangible meaning. She was disappointed by this for many reasons, but fortunately found resolution, although not through Clarksdale Medical Supplies.

Rita is an elderly woman who is in reasonably good health. Unfortunately, her husband, Benjamin, does not have the same health status. Very frail, he has been wheelchair bound for 2 years. Rita, ever concerned for his comfort, routinely searches for anything and everything that will ease his pain, improve mobility, and permit him to live as peaceful and comfortable a life as possible.

In recent weeks, Rita had noticed a number of television advertisements for Clarksdale Medical Supplies, promoting a new wheelchair that promised to provide industry-leading comfort. It is made by a manufacturer known as Medical Star, a fairly new company that uses space-age materials and ergonomically engineered designs to optimize comfort, support, and maneuverability in its mobility products. Given the newness of the manufacturer, Rita had never purchased a product made by Medical Star, nor was its distribution network terribly well developed. But she just learned, courtesy of recent television advertisements, that Clarksdale Medical Supplies sells Medical Star's products, including its new line of innovative wheelchairs.

Rita had never conducted business with Clarksdale Medical Supplies, but was familiar with the store, as it heavily advertises its product offerings on television, radio, and in newspapers in Clarksdale. She previously had always opted to purchase her husband's durable medical equipment through a local pharmacy retailer, Castlewood Discount Drugs, largely due to her long-standing business relationship with its owner, Randall Turner. However, Castlewood Discount Drugs currently does not offer the Medical Star line, leading her to consider extending patronage to Clarksdale Medical Supplies.

Rita and her husband are not particularly wealthy, and they have no children to provide financial assistance in cases of emergency, so the two must make every dollar count, leading her to be notoriously careful about where patronage is extended. Rita, however, was relatively comfortable with the idea of purchasing from Clarksdale Medical Supplies because the company so passionately communicates that it offers only top-quality brands, the best service and support, no questions asked returns, and is totally committed to customer satisfaction. In researching the store online, she learned that it had a lengthy history in Clarksdale, dating back 2 decades, something that was not surprising given that she long recalled the establishment's advertisements. The store was owned and operated by Troy Irving, Clarksdale Medical Supplies founder, who also was a native of the city. The store's Web site listed a number of customer testimonials, all showering Clarksdale Medical Supplies with high praise for the excellent care and attention extended. With any reservations to do business with Clarksdale Medical Supplies dismissed by the content of both the store's advertising messages and its Web site, Rita and Benjamin decided to pay the store a visit.

Making her way into the establishment with her husband, the two were greeted by Troy who worked very hard to evaluate Benjamin's needs, providing demonstrations of Medical Star's wheelchair models. After a bit of trial and error, a particular model was identified, tested by Benjamin, and ultimately purchased. Both Rita and Benjamin were extremely impressed by Troy's enthusiasm and assistance throughout the transaction. The two departed the store with the new Medical Star wheelchair and returned home.

Over the next few days, the wheelchair performed as expected, living up to the bold claims of comfort, support, and maneuverability. But by the second week of use, its left wheel developed some resistance, as if something internally was catching the mechanism and preventing the wheel from freely spinning. Rita was not terribly concerned, because the wheelchair had a lifetime warranty from the manufacturer. More comforting, however, was that it was purchased from the locally owned and operated Clarksdale Medical Supplies. Rita recalled the store's generous policies on customer satisfaction, as promoted in its advertisements, and was certain that the matter would quickly be remedied.

The following morning, Rita telephoned Troy at Clarksdale Medical Supplies and informed him that Benjamin's Medical Star wheelchair was experiencing a wheel problem. To keep things as simple and trouble free as possible, Rita requested that the store exchange the broken wheelchair for a new one. Troy, however, responded that she should contact Medical Star's toll-free telephone number to arrange for the unit to be shipped to a repair facility, after which the wheelchair would be repaired appropriately or, if repairs were not possible, replaced. In turn, Rita communicated that she preferred to handle this locally and, again, requested a replacement and reminded Troy that Clarksdale Medical Supplies advertises a 30-day unconditional money back guarantee if customers are not 100% satisfied. She indicated that she indeed was not 100% satisfied and asked Troy to honor the guarantee. Troy, however, stood firm, noting that Medical Star would be happy to address her concerns. He repeated the manufacturer's telephone number and abruptly concluded the telephone call.

Rita could not believe what had just happened. Not only was Troy a completely different person after the sale than he was before the sale, demonstrating to her that his kindness was feigned in an attempt to generate a sale, but his actions were completely going against the words of his advertisements. Rita felt as though she and Benjamin had been swindled by an insincere businessman and his profit-hungry business.

Rita wanted to fight, but she simply did not have the time or energy to file a complaint with local or national consumer advocacy groups, nor did she have the time to more formally take up matters with Troy and Clarksdale Medical Supplies. Further, she could not very well ship the wheelchair back to Medical Star, because this would leave Benjamin with nothing. Her personal limitations were weighing down on her ability to seek resolution and her obligations to attending to her frail husband did not help matters. She felt as though her husband would simply have to make do with the faulty wheelchair.

Several days pass with no improvements in the wheelchair when Rita suddenly had an idea. Perhaps she could contact Randall at Castlewood Discount Drugs and request assistance. He might be able to fix the wheelchair onsite. Sure, Castlewood Discount Drugs does not carry the Medical Star line, but the store does sell durable medical equipment and might possibly be able to troubleshoot the problem. Rita was reluctant to contact Randall, given that she bought the wheelchair from one of his competitors, but she felt as though she had no other option.

That afternoon, Rita telephoned Randall, explained the situation, and requested assistance. Randall noted that the Medical Star line was new and unproven, leading him to forgo carrying the product line until he learned more about product quality. He suggested that Benjamin try a particular model that Castlewood Discount Drugs carried, noting that if he and Rita were satisfied, he would simply offer it in exchange for the defective Medical Star wheelchair. Rita was relieved and welcomed his offer. Randall himself loaded the new wheelchair, visited Rita and Benjamin at their residence, made the wheelchair exchange, and all was well.

On leaving the residence, Rita profusely thanked Randall. Still, she was concerned that perhaps he had been too generous. Randall indicated that, yes, he likely would only be able to resell the Medical Star wheelchair as a used model, assuming that it could be refurbished, but that did not matter to him. He communicated that given her longtime patronage of Castlewood Discount Drugs, exchanging the wheelchair was his way of demonstrating his appreciation. Rita promised that she would never extend her patronage to another store.

DISCUSSION

1. Rita was highly dissatisfied with the treatment that she and her husband received from Troy and Clarksdale Medical Supplies. Although she decided against taking any sort of action against the store, what options are available in such circumstances? Of the options listed, if you were in Rita's position, which one would you choose and why?

2. Rita and Troy clearly disagreed over the appropriate remedy for the defective wheelchair. Based on the information supplied in the case, who was right? Be sure to justify your response.

3. Some retail establishments do just as Clarksdale Medical Supplies did, by requiring that customers return defective items, even immediately after purchase, to regional repair centers rather than to the particular establishment that made the sale. What are your thoughts on this retailing practice? What motivations do you anticipate to be behind this practice?

4. At its core, this case is about an establishment that says one thing, via marketing communications and salesmanship, but does another. While the case presents an extreme example, it is not uncommon for establishments to be tall on words and short on actions. Discuss the importance of following words with actions. Then, describe an experience where you personally encountered words that were not followed with actions. How did it make you feel? What did you do?

5. At the conclusion of the case, Rita turns to Randall and Castlewood Discount Drugs for assistance in remedying her problem. Even though Castlewood Discount Drugs did not carry the Medical Star line, Randall still accepted the wheelchair, replacing it with a brand new competing model. He was destined to take a loss, but did so to demonstrate appreciation for Rita's longtime patronage. Discuss the risks and returns associated with Randall's generosity. Although this particular case deals with healthcare goods, how might the same generosity be replicated with healthcare services? Would you embrace the philosophy exhibited by Randall and Castlewood Discount Drugs? Why or why not?

24

The Onsite Advertising Agent

SNAPSHOT

Institution:
Shepherd Medical Center, a 330-bed, not-for-profit establishment providing general medical and surgical services

Location:
Ridgeland (population 228,775), located in the Mountain region of the United States

Characters:
Ms. Glenda Bailey, Vice President of Marketing
Mr. Michael Simmons, President and Chief Executive Officer
(both of Shepherd Medical Center)

Context:
In this case, the newly hired top executive of a medical center discovers that the establishment's marketing operations are incomplete, requiring major upgrades if his vision is to become a reality.

Michael Simmons, newly hired President and Chief Executive Officer of Shepherd Medical Center, is about to shake things up. In his first few days as leader of the medical center, he has witnessed a number of very concerning issues pertaining to administrative operations that ultimately are hampering institutional productivity and resulting market share gains. One area of particular weakness is that of marketing, which is not delivering value across its core disciplinary components. Given that Michael knows that excellent marketing performance is essential for institutional success, he has decided to place pressure on the current Vice President of Marketing, Glenda Bailey, to improve the depth and breadth of marketing operations immediately.

Situated in Ridgeland, a city of 228,775 residents situated in the Mountain region of the United States, Shepherd Medical Center is a 330-bed, not-for-profit establishment providing general medical and surgical services. The institution is ranked a distant fourth in market share, falling well behind the three predominant competitors in the marketplace. Twenty years ago, Shepherd Medical Center was the undisputed market leader in Ridgeland, but a revolving door of poor leaders and many bad decisions led to its current status as an underperforming healthcare entity. With a new governing board having been appointed recently, Shepherd Medical Center is looking to return to its past days of market leadership and, as such, hired Michael.

Michael is an energetic healthcare executive who has always strived for excellence. He has progressively worked his way up the ranks of administration, earning his Master of Health Administration and several certifications along the way, and was hired by Shepherd Medical Center primarily to revitalize operations for the purpose of building market share. Michael, a competitor to the core, is no stranger to such challenges, having gained a reputation as a turnaround expert after bringing prosperity back to several ill-performing healthcare facilities. He is excited about the challenges and opportunities at Shepherd Medical Center but knows that tough decisions must be made.

While Michael has educated himself in virtually every area of health administration, he well knows that he cannot personally address every single matter at Shepherd Medical Center, understanding that he must delegate various duties and responsibilities to capable senior managers. Knowing that he must have an effective executive management team to embrace and implement his vision for a prosperous future and associated market share conquests, he decided to perform an introductory assessment of the skills and abilities of Shepherd Medical Center's current senior management staff via a series of informational interviews.

Because marketing will play an integral role in building market share for Shepherd Medical Center, Michael decided to begin his senior management team interviews by meeting with Glenda, who has held the marketing leadership position at the establishment for 9 years. A believer that departmental operations are to entail the entire scope of marketing, as formally defined, Michael chose to hold the meeting in Glenda's office in order to get a better feel for the department's production and culture, and to lead by example that executives must not be bound to their given offices.

On arrival, Michael was quick to take note of departmental activities, witnessing marketing staffers hard at work on the preparation and submission of telephone directory listings for the medical center's various constituencies, including its medical staff. He also noted various pieces of artwork that have either been deployed or are being considered for deployment in advertising and other marketing communications messages.

As the two initiated their meeting, Michael commented on the various marketing communications activities taking place in the department and asked for further details. He first inquired about the particular marketing communications used by Shepherd Medical Center and the mechanisms for calculating return on investment. Glenda responded by noting that the medical center generally employed advertising and direct marketing to reach its target audiences. Billboards mostly were used, supplemented periodically by newspaper advertisements and occasionally by radio and television advertisements. Direct marketing generally involved direct mail pieces featuring various elements of Shepherd Medical Center's service array that were sent to community residents.

Glenda went on to discuss Shepherd Medical Center's public relations efforts, noting that her department actively forwarded press releases to various media outlets to announce new services and newly hired physicians and other caregivers. Open houses and health education classes were often held in an effort to generate positive word-of-mouth communications. Further, she handled all press inquiries and attended civic events on behalf of the medical center. Sales promotion was occasionally used, primarily through the distribution of free gifts, such as Shepherd Medical Center t-shirts, pens, refrigerator magnets, and the like, all in an effort to keep the establishment's brand name at the top of patients' minds.

Michael genuinely was impressed with Glenda's marketing communications knowledge and her efforts to positively present Shepherd Medical Center in the marketplace seemed well placed, but her explanations regarding return on investment did not meet his expectations. Glenda's calculations were more akin to informal guesstimates than efforts to scientifically determine generated return. Rather than focusing on outcomes of various marketing communications efforts, Glenda focused on the circulation figures associated with given communicative mechanisms. But Michael well knew that reach and frequency merely provide indications of exposure levels and were not firm indicators of bankable returns. His concerns began to mount.

Asking about other elements of marketing, Glenda had little to offer. She did not engage in formal environmental analysis activities, nor did she assemble and maintain any strategic guidance tools, such as marketing dashboards. Marketing research at Shepherd Medical Center was nonexistent, with the exception of patient satisfaction surveys that were occasionally circulated, but even these were administered by the nursing service department, with a consulting firm supplying the analytics. Efforts at new product development were equally dismal. Clearly, Shepherd Medical Center's marketing department would better be described as a communications department, much of which could be handled by a competent advertising agency.

This simply was not good enough for Michael. While he was disappointed with the production value and capabilities of Glenda's department, he was not entirely surprised by his findings. He knew that Shepherd Medical Center's shallow market share in the community probably resulted from multiple inadequacies, with lack of marketing rigor being an obvious weakness. He also knew that it was not terribly uncommon for hospital marketing operations to be, in many cases, glorified onsite advertising agencies, which provide only a sliver of marketing services.

Michael politely communicated to Glenda that his expectations for Shepherd Medical Center's marketing unit entailed much more than that which the department was providing under her leadership. He further communicated that attainment of his vision was based largely on Shepherd Medical Center's marketing success and that he needed the department to deliver everything that the discipline of marketing has to offer. Michael then instructed Glenda to prepare a plan for upgrading operations, giving her 2 weeks to present this to him.

As Michael made his way back to his office, he was unsure whether Glenda would be able to deliver a comprehensive marketing department on behalf of Shepherd Medical Center, given her responses to his questions on comprehensive marketing operations. Knowing that her educational background was in graphic design and not the broader discipline of marketing did not provide him with any further comfort. A tough decision likely awaits.

DISCUSSION

1. Michael indicated that he believed that tapping the power of the discipline of marketing would be essential for Shepherd Medical Center to regain prominence as a medical institution in Ridgeland. Prepare a narrative discussing the importance of marketing to the success of overall business operations in healthcare entities.

2. Shepherd Medical Center's marketing operations clearly did not measure up to Michael's expectations. Although the case notes a few neglected areas, prepare a comprehensive list of areas and associated activities of marketing that Glenda was neglecting in her role as Vice President of Marketing. Be sure to consult a good marketing definition and textbook as you go about itemizing deficiencies in Shepherd Medical Center's marketing department.

3. While Glenda handled marketing communications very well, she did not handle return on investment calculations appropriately. Comment on why her approach to return on investment was inadequate and offer suggestions for measuring the value of the marketing communications that Shepherd Medical Center deployed.

4. As the case concludes, Michael expresses doubts that Glenda possesses the educational background to provide comprehensive marketing services on behalf of Shepherd Medical Center, viewing her training as a graphic designer to be too limited. Do you think Michael's concerns regarding her educational background are with or without merit? Why do you believe this to be the case?

5. Michael indicated that he was not surprised by the state of Shepherd Medical Center's marketing department, noting that he had seen departments in other institutions that were equally limited. What are your thoughts on the degree to which healthcare organizations are getting the full benefit of the discipline of marketing?

CHAPTER 25

Making the Intangible, Tangible

SNAPSHOT

Institutions:
Summit Sports Medicine Clinic, a nine-physician, multispecialty sports medicine practice
Burbank Lions, a minor league baseball team

Location:
Burbank (population 805,605), located in the East North Central region of the United States

Characters:
Dr. Gregory Cannon, Co-Owner and Physician
Dr. Jacob Douglas, Co-Owner and Physician
Mr. Gordon Henderson, Administrator
Ms. Amy Zimmerman, Assistant Administrator
(all of Summit Sports Medicine Clinic)

Context:
In this case, the newly hired assistant administrator of a sports medicine clinic plans to add a tangible component to the intangible patient experience in an effort to improve brand identity.

Amy Zimmerman, newly hired Assistant Administrator of Summit Sports Medicine Clinic, is ready to make a positive contribution. She has just learned of a monthly contest sponsored by the clinic that seeks suggestions for improvement, providing a reward to the employee submitting the best idea. Although Amy is new at the establishment, the contest and its benefits, both for the clinic as well as herself, are proving to be very motivational. She intends to keep an eye open for opportunities hiding in plain sight, as well as those that are more elusive in an effort to improve operations at Summit Sports Medicine Clinic.

This is Amy's first professional employment position, but she is very familiar with medical office operations, courtesy of her prior experience as a medical assistant. She recently earned an Associate of Arts in Business Administration from a local community college and is currently enrolled in a Bachelor of Business Administration program, attending during the evenings. Amy plans eventually to move into upper management capacities in hospitals and understands how valuable the experience at Summit Sports Medicine Clinic will be in helping her to realize higher career goals.

Summit Sports Medicine Clinic, a nine-physician, multispecialty sports medicine practice offering services running the gamut of sports-related medical care, is based in Burbank, a city of 805,605 located in the East North Central region of the United States. Established just 6 years ago, Summit Sports Medicine Clinic is a fairly new clinic, but has quickly earned a reputation as a high-quality sports medicine provider, primarily serving the population in and around a wealthy area of the city.

Over the past couple of weeks, Amy has been completing her new employee orientation, learning about the operations of the establishment under the guidance of Summit Sports Medicine Clinic's Administrator, Gordon Henderson. In previous days of orientation, Amy has learned a great deal about the particular philosophy embraced by the clinic. Her indoctrination included, among other things, detailed meetings with Summit Sports Medicine Clinic's owners and founders, Drs. Gregory Cannon and Jacob Douglas, in which they expressed their guiding philosophy that nothing is ever good enough; that there is always room for improvement. In fact, Drs. Cannon and Douglas largely attribute Summit Sports Medicine Clinic's success to this philosophy, as continual improvements yield continual benefits for patients, improving retention and generating loyalty.

To ensure that this philosophy resonated with all employees, the two physicians incorporated mechanisms that encourage Summit Sports

Medicine Clinic's staff members to think outside of the box, investigating new ways to further enhance the clinic and resulting patient experiences. One such mechanism entailed a monthly contest that was initiated to encourage improvement, problem resolution, and otherwise serve to motivate employees, rewarding the employee submitting the most innovative and ingenious idea.

Gordon confirmed that the contest had made a positive impact at the clinic, with several suggestions being incorporated for significant gains. One suggestion recommended the addition of a canopy to cover the walkway leading to the clinic to keep patients dry on rainy days as they walked in for their appointments. Another involved making better use of the Internet, permitting patients to, for example, schedule appointments online and receive reminders of upcoming appointments via email and text messages. Gordon also noted that the contest was proving to be very motivational, with all of Summit Sports Medicine Clinic's employees eagerly awaiting announcements of monthly winners and their associated ideas. Amy agreed, noting that it certainly was encouraging her to think about methods of improvement.

Completing her orientation period, Amy entered the weekend, with much of her time being devoted to studying Summit Sports Medicine Clinic's various policies and procedures. In the back of her mind, she, too, was thinking of possible improvement initiatives. By late Saturday afternoon, she was exhausted and, realizing the need for a break, she decided to attend the local minor league team's baseball game. As Amy entered the stadium, courtesy of it being baseball night at the park, she was given a baseball bearing the logo of the home team, the Burbank Lions. Making her way to her reserved seat, it suddenly struck her that Summit Sports Medicine Clinic could adopt a similar approach.

The parallels actually were fairly prominent, Amy believed. Both the Burbank Lions and Summit Sports Medicine Clinic were in the service delivery business. Customers extend their patronage and, in return, they receive some sort of experience—entertainment in the case of the Burbank Lions, medical care in the case of Summit Sports Medicine Clinic. When the experiences are over—hopefully a victory in the case of the Burbank Lions and improved health status in the case of Summit Sports Medicine Clinic—customers typically do not leave with anything tangible.

But the Burbank Lions brought a degree of tangibility to the intangible by providing a baseball bearing its team logo to ballpark patrons. This not only served as a branded reminder of the team but also developed a feeling of good will. Amy believed that this might be a great practice for Summit Sports Medicine Clinic to adopt.

On returning home, Amy's satisfaction with her idea grew. She had seen clinics provide free gifts, like branded calendars and refrigerator magnets, but these lacked a feeling of substance, likely minimizing patient attention and appreciation. Given this, she set out to think of an affordable, tangible offering that was substantive, unique, and capable of being branded with Summit Sports Medicine Clinic's logo that could be given to patients in appreciation of their patronage.

Showing up to work bright and early on Monday morning, Amy decided to ask Gordon for insights as to whether he could see value in submitting her idea as a contest entry. Gordon was very impressed with Amy's suggestion, noting that the free gift would have substantial marketing value, generating goodwill, shoring up patronage, and, if the gift was well conceived, could serve as a unique product differentiator. Much to Amy's satisfaction, Gordon requested that she reduce her idea to writing and enter it in Summit Sports Medicine Clinic's monthly contest.

Amy did so, carefully describing her idea to bring a degree of tangibility to the intangible offering of medical services. She provided details regarding the Burbank Lions example and also reflected on other examples she recalled from the past, noting that Summit Sports Medicine Clinic might very well witness benefits from the provision of free gifts to patients. She then submitted her idea.

At month's end, as had become a tradition at the clinic, Gordon called all employees into the lobby area just before opening for the day to announce the contest winner. From all of the month's entries, Amy's idea was selected. For her idea, Amy received a certificate of appreciation and a check for $100, along with recognition from her fellow employees. Gordon, along with Drs. Cannon and Douglas, congratulated Amy on her victory and issued an associated challenge. Specifically, they wanted her to develop a list of suggestions for the free gift. They encouraged her not to worry with budget matters at the moment; instead, concentrate on ideas that would not be obviously cost prohibitive, but would have real meaning and value from the patient's perspective. Amy already had developed a brief list of criteria—something substantive, unique, and capable of being branded—and welcomed the new challenge.

DISCUSSION

1. The case describes a monthly contest held by Summit Sports Medicine Clinic that seeks suggestions for improvement, rewarding employees who submit winning ideas. From the case, it seems that Summit Sports Medicine Clinic's leaders are pleased with the results. What are your thoughts on such a contest and what impact would you expect the contest to have on both employee and patient experiences?

2. Summit Sports Medicine Clinic's founders, Drs. Cannon and Douglas, proclaimed their guiding philosophy to be that nothing is ever good enough; that there is always room for improvement. Do you agree with their philosophy? Why or why not?

3. Giving free gifts to customers has long since been a practice in business and industry. In your local market, examine what types of free gifts companies currently are offering to their clients. For those gifts that are provided by companies outside of the healthcare industry, do any of them make sense for use by healthcare entities? Why or why not?

4. After winning the contest, Amy was asked to develop a list of gift suggestions for Summit Sports Medicine Clinic's patients. Thinking of the case and of the criteria noted for the gift, prepare a list of five potential items that Summit Sports Medicine Clinic might consider gifting. Please discuss your reasons for making each selection and note each gift's anticipated benefits. Of all of the gifts that you noted, which one would you choose and why?

5. Assume that the gift you selected in Inquiry 4 was deemed acceptable by the leadership of Summit Sports Medicine Clinic. Identify a vendor who could supply this particular gift and also investigate associated pricing. Describe the gift in detail and indicate your plans for attaching brand identity. How would you go about distributing the gift to patients of the clinic? How might the clinic use the gift in other ways to build patronage?

26

Opening Minds

SNAPSHOT

Institution:
Knightsbridge Health System, a for-profit, 1575-bed health system consisting of six medical centers providing general medical and surgical services

Location:
Laurel (population 594,210), located in the East South Central region of the United States

Characters:
Mr. Kevin Foster, Chief Marketing Officer
Ms. Dana Sutherland, Chief Executive Officer
(both of Knightsbridge Health System)

Context:
In this case, the top marketing executive of a health system recommends an innovative method for improving the patient experience by introducing retail elements into the servicescape.

Kevin Foster, Chief Marketing Officer at Knightsbridge Health System, is excited. Several weeks ago he was asked to join an architectural planning committee to discuss the design and construction of Knightsbridge Health System's newest hospital, Knightsbridge-Eastgate Medical Center. Kevin is new to Knightsbridge Health System, taking the position as marketing chief just 3 months ago, but he has worked quickly to learn the operations of his new organization and was honored to be selected to serve on the planning committee.

This is Kevin's first opportunity to serve at the helm of a marketing department, but his education and former employment positions have prepared him well for the role. Kevin entered marketing through a less traditional route. Instead of earning a college degree in marketing or business administration, he pursued a degree in commercial art and entered marketing on the creative side, preparing artwork for several advertising agencies before moving into his first management position in sales, working for an apparel company with retail outlets in shopping malls across America. Eventually becoming the company's national sales manager, over the course of his retail service, he acquired a Master of Business Administration to broaden his knowledge of marketing and other business disciplines. With 15 years of experience under his belt, he was ready for a change, applied for the Knightsbridge Health System Chief Marketing Officer position, and was awarded the opportunity.

Knightsbridge Health System comprises six medical centers having a total of 1575 licensed beds. It is located in Laurel, a city of 594,210 residents located in the East South Central region of the United States. The for-profit health system operates medical centers in all but one region of the city—Eastgate—an area that has witnessed significant growth in recent years as the population of Laurel expands. Knightsbridge-Eastgate Medical Center, Knightsbridge Health System's seventh property that will add 250 beds to the system's total, will fill this void and afford Knightsbridge Health System with total market coverage in Laurel.

Knightsbridge Health System embraces a moderately conservative approach to healthcare delivery, emphasizing traditional positives such as high-quality care, employee excellence, and devotion to a guiding mission that focuses on patient attention, care, respect, and shareholder value. But the system is not afraid to take chances, and, as such, has the gained the reputation of being an innovator, at least within the local healthcare marketplace. Still, Knightsbridge Health System almost never looks outside of the healthcare industry for proven practices from other industries that could be adopted or adapted for gains, something not terribly atypical in the healthcare industry.

Kevin, however, is one who views marketing practices, regardless of industry of origin and use, to be fair game for incorporation into any setting, including health care. From his perspective, the trick is to cast one's net broadly, searching for innovative ideas across business and industry. Then, assess their feasibility for use in the healthcare industry, investigating if they can be adopted outright or adapted without losing the characteristics that made the practices successful in other industries. Kevin readily acknowledges the unique nature of the healthcare industry in comparison to other industries, but with zeal, creativity, and improvisation, he views many gains, already tested and proven elsewhere, to be capable of incorporation in the healthcare environment for massive benefits to patients and the healthcare entities that serve them.

As a member of the architectural planning committee, Kevin has been exposed to many discussions regarding Knightsbridge-Eastgate Medical Center, with his greatest interest pertaining to the design and functionality of the servicescape, the physical setting of the facility from parking to landscaping to facility signage to ergonomics to employee attire and beyond. Mostly observing and providing occasional commentary, Kevin was surprised in a recent meeting when Dana Sutherland, Knightsbridge Health System's Chief Executive Officer, asked him for insights that would take Knightsbridge-Eastgate Medical Center's servicescape to the next level. Seeking to tap into Kevin's diverse background and newness to both Knightsbridge Health System and the healthcare industry, she specifically wanted perspectives from someone who, unlike everyone else sitting around the conference table, had experience outside of the healthcare industry, and Kevin fit the bill.

Kevin was flattered by Dana's request and, as luck would have it, he had already conceptualized a unique servicescape that, just as Dana was seeking, changed the rules of servicescape design in the healthcare sector. As the team rookie, he had been somewhat hesitant to share his vision, but with Dana's request, he was afforded the perfect opportunity to present his ideas.

Kevin communicated that his vision was unique to health care but not to another industry with very similar attributes—the transportation industry, with airports serving as the primary model. At airports, passengers essentially are captive and the wait times for flight departures, even when they are operating on schedule, are often lengthy. The same hardships exist in healthcare institutions with patients being captives who often face lengthy waits before being seen by caregivers. Just as in airports, family members often accompany their loved ones to healthcare institutions, bringing yet another party into the service venue.

Kevin went on to communicate that airports have responded to this by incorporating retail operations that permit waits to be less frustrating and potentially even productive for captive audiences. Modern airports, especially those in large cities, incorporate shopping opportunities, restaurants, video arcades, and art galleries, among many other things to enhance the travel experience. These establishments typically are not operated by the airports themselves, but rather by companies that lease space from the airports, providing a revenue source, in addition to passenger benefit.

Kevin thought that given the obvious parallels, healthcare entities could do the same, incorporating retail elements for a vastly improved servicescape and potentially even generating revenue for healthcare providers. He echoed that this, of course, would go well beyond the standard hospital gift shop or cafeteria, but since Knightsbridge-Eastgate Medical Center was still on the drawing board, the system had the perfect opportunity to do something innovative.

At the conclusion of Kevin's presentation of his vision, some of the audience members chuckled, reminding him that Knightsbridge Health System was in the business of health care, not retailing. But they were quickly silenced when Dana applauded Kevin for thinking in a very innovative way and expressed that his idea clearly had merit. She went on to say that his vision not only would benefit patients and potentially the medical center's bottom line, but, if done well, it would represent an unbelievably robust product differentiation tool.

As the meeting drew to a close, Dana challenged Kevin to refine his idea, requesting for the forthcoming meeting a detailed plan and, tapping into his skill as a graphic designer, associated servicescape illustrations. Excited by the positive feedback and upcoming challenge, Kevin thought to himself that this was an excellent way to begin his healthcare career.

DISCUSSION

1. Kevin's prior experience in other work environments led him to formulate a vision that was very different than that which is typically seen in the healthcare industry. Do you believe his vision for merging retail and health services is viable for medical service providers such as Knightsbridge-Eastgate Medical Center? Why or why not?

2. Regardless of your thoughts on the viability or lack thereof of Kevin's vision, what does this case say about the practice of looking across industries, regardless of scope or mission, for innovations that might be applicable in the healthcare industry?

3. With healthcare executives subscribing to the same healthcare industry journals, being members of the same healthcare trade and professional organizations, attending conferences all focused on the healthcare industry, and possessing similar educational backgrounds, their focus exclusively on industry occurrences is not surprising. What would you recommend that healthcare executives do to ensure that they have exposure to other industries and associated innovations?

4. Take a moment to reflect deeply on customer experiences that you have had outside of the healthcare industry. Then, identify at least one practice that might be borrowed by healthcare entities to benefit patients. Be sure to share the details of this practice, which industry it came from, and how you plan to initiate it in the healthcare industry.

5. After presenting his vision, Kevin experienced a period of slight ridicule by some of his colleagues who chuckled at his idea before they were silenced by Dana's response. Bold new directions are always going to face ridicule and objection by status quo executives and managers, but they at least should be shared as each has the potential to yield results. Still, the possibility of ridicule often prevents individuals with innovative ideas from coming forward, which, at least in some cases, results in brilliant ideas going to waste. What steps would you take to ensure that individuals in your organization feel comfortable sharing innovative ideas?

CHAPTER 27

Advertising Does Work

SNAPSHOT

Institution:
Lucerne Hospital, a 275-bed, for-profit establishment providing general medical and surgical services

Location:
Gladstone (population 367,302), located in the South Atlantic region of the United States

Characters:
Ms. Betty Albertson, Director of Laboratory Services
Ms. Julie Callahan, Vice President of Marketing
Mr. Roy Fields, Vice President of Clinical Operations
Mr. Craig Turner, President and Chief Executive Officer
(all of Lucerne Hospital)

Context:
In this case, a laboratory services director questions her establishment's investment in advertising and receives a much-needed lesson.

Driving across town, Betty Albertson, Director of Laboratory Services at Lucerne Hospital, is becoming increasingly agitated. On her 7-mile route from her residence to work, she hears two radio commercials for her hospital, counts seven of its billboard advertisements, observes three bus shelters promoting the hospital, and passes four taxis, each plastered with her establishment's logo. Her agitation stems from the fact that she views all of the advertising conducted by her employer to be very wasteful. From her perspective, it would be better to place the funds used to pay for these advertisements into patient care rather than into the coffers of television and radio stations, outdoor advertising companies, and the like. As she continues to see promotional displays across every conceivable form of media, her frustrations are increasing and she has begun to act out on these tensions, poisoning morale in the hospital and harming her very own reputation.

Lucerne Hospital is a 275-bed, for-profit provider of general medical and surgical services. It is based in Gladstone, a city of 367,302 residents, located in the South Atlantic region of the United States. As is the case in most metropolitan areas, Gladstone's seven major medical establishments are intensely involved in the battle for market share with each other. At present, Lucerne Hospital is the market leader in the city, holding the first-place position by a healthy margin of several percentage points, with the remaining six establishments being grouped in close proximity to one another with slight distinctions in their given market share percentages.

Betty has been employed at Lucerne Hospital for approximately 2 years, acquiring her position as Director of Laboratory Services, after over 25 years of service in various clinical and administrative positions associated with laboratory services in other medical institutions. She is an aggressive employee who strives to deliver the best service possible for patients and the many departments that look to Lucerne Hospital's laboratory for assistance in care delivery. Betty, however, does have the tendency to occasionally become too passionate regarding her various perspectives and beliefs, leading to difficulties with other staff members and departments in the hospital. Betty only possesses training in the biological sciences, but holds natural administrative capabilities that have vaulted her into positions of leadership, albeit in clinical services departments at the level of middle management.

Betty's frustrations over Lucerne Hospital's involvement in advertising only recently emerged, coming to the forefront following a denial that she received, rejecting her request to upgrade some of the equipment in the hospital's laboratory. The denial was issued by Craig Turner, Lucerne Hospital's President and Chief Executive Officer, based on his executive committee's perspective that the upgrades desired by Betty were unwarranted and wasteful in that the laboratory already possessed modern, properly functioning equipment that was, in fact, more advanced than that possessed by any competitor in the city.

Failing to grasp the essence of the rejection—that there essentially was not a business justification for upgrading—Betty made the assumption that the hospital simply could not afford to purchase the equipment due to encumbrances elsewhere. Instead of accepting the response from Craig's office, Betty began complaining openly and notoriously in the presence of her staff members and others in the hospital, criticizing hospital expenditures on myriad fronts. She reserved her most caustic criticisms for Lucerne Hospital's advertising as she could see no reason for placing the given promotional messages. She believed that they had no impact on the hospital or its market position and simply stood to take money away from patient care.

Betty's fury reached its peak when she happened to meet an advertising sales representative at a social event in Gladstone. Although the representative did not service the account of Lucerne Hospital, Betty asked for a rough estimate of the advertising expenses that likely were incurred given the media typically deployed by the establishment. The response nearly knocked Betty off of her feet, as she learned, among other things, that some of the billboards leased by the hospital were as high as $3000 per month, with the television campaigns being even more expensive. Betty was enraged.

With that information, Betty grew increasingly bitter and was quick to share her negative perspectives with her fellow employees while at work, during breaks in the hospital's cafeteria, and even out in the community. Her criticisms were not only becoming more pronounced, they also were beginning to offend some of Lucerne Hospital's staff members who were annoyed at Betty's constant negativity. Unfortunately, her negativity had proved to be somewhat contagious, acting to demoralize and incite anger in at least some of her coworkers. As one would imagine, it did not take long for news of Betty's unprofessional behavior to reach Craig and his executive officers.

Craig was a take-charge person who, on learning that a member of Lucerne Hospital's management team was speaking against hospital practices, called for an immediate meeting with Betty, her supervisor,

Roy Fields, who serves as the Vice President of Clinical Operations, and, as Betty's source of frustration pertained to advertising, Julie Callahan, the hospital's Vice President of Marketing. Craig directly confronted Betty, criticizing her for letting her emotions run wild following the earlier rejection of her request for new laboratory equipment, and denigrating her for spreading her angst to other employees. While he was not required to justify the hospital's use of advertising to Betty, Craig used the opportunity to educate her in hopes that it would enlighten her and make her a better employee and manager.

Craig proceeded to provide a history of Lucerne Hospital under his 15-year tenure at the facility, noting that, at one point during the early part of his career at the establishment, the hospital occupied last place in the battle for market share. Currently, he noted that Lucerne Hospital occupies the market leadership position, achieving this prominent place 5 years ago, with increases in its lead occurring every year since. He credits the achievement of market leadership to the hospital's ability to (1) offer the best healthcare products in the marketplace and (2) communicate effectively with target audiences. He viewed it to be essential to deliver on both product quality and communications fronts. Lucerne Hospital delivered on both points, yielding a very prosperous establishment.

Craig then asked Julie, as the institution's top marketing executive, to discuss the hospital's advertising and its benefits. Julie did so, presenting her methods for formulating the marketing communications mix, her rationale for purchasing advertising across various media, and her methods for measuring the results derived from given investments. While advertising alone did not result in Lucerne Hospital's success, it certainly played a prominent role, especially in the area of bolstering patient volume across certain product lines, many of which directly impacted and benefited laboratory services.

Craig communicated that the totality of efforts provided across administrative and clinical operations resulted in the success experienced by Lucerne Hospital. He indicated that great products must be well communicated to target audiences. Failures in either the product area or in the communications area will yield negative business results.

Wrapping up the meeting, Craig conveyed that the rejection denying Betty's request to purchase new laboratory equipment was based not on costs, but on her request's lack of merit. For future reference, he encouraged Betty to ensure that she possessed a thorough understanding of the situation at hand before resorting to criticisms and to be especially careful when criticizing something that she knew utterly nothing about.

DISCUSSION

1. In this case, Betty directs anger at Lucerne Hospital's involvement in advertising, viewing it to be consuming resources that otherwise could be directed toward patient care. Although the basis of her anger is questionable, as it seems to be motivated by the denial of her recent request to purchase new laboratory equipment, her perspectives of the wastefulness of advertising are not terribly uncommon for some working in the healthcare industry. What are your thoughts on advertising in the healthcare industry? Is it wasteful? Why or why not?

2. Addressing Betty's unprofessional behavior, Craig takes the opportunity to enlighten her regarding the role that advertising has played in Lucerne Hospital's success. This is complemented by Julie's presentation of information associated with selecting and monitoring the establishment's marketing communications. It certainly seems as though Lucerne Hospital is scientifically managing the marketing function, ensuring that investments are delivering adequate returns. However, many healthcare institutions do not address marketing in this fashion, with money being thrown at advertising without any formal measurement system being in place to ensure appropriate return on investment. What are your thoughts on purchasing advertising without ensuring that its return on investment is monitored? Do you believe that this practice gives the entire discipline of marketing a bad name? Be sure to justify your responses.

3. Ralph Waldo Emerson is quoted as saying, "Build a better mousetrap and the world will beat a path to your door." This is sometimes used motivationally by those seeking business success, yet it conflicts with Craig's perspective that success requires effective products, coupled with effective communications. What are your thoughts on Craig's perspective as a formula for marketing success? Would you add or subtract anything from this simple formula? Why or why not?

4. Betty clearly possessed no understanding of the strategic and tactical importance of Lucerne Hospital's marketing practices. Although Betty's ignorance, coupled with her unprofessional behavior, caused her to lose credibility, the case does cause one to consider ensuring that all employees of given healthcare establishments understand the strategic and tactical importance of various institutional operations. What are your thoughts on this practice? How might you go about operationalizing this practice in a healthcare organization?

5. What are your thoughts on the manner in which Craig addressed Betty? Would you have done anything differently? Why or why not?

CHAPTER 28

Dead Celebrities

SNAPSHOT

Institution:
Carthage Mobility, a manufacturer and distributor of personal mobility products

Location:
Carthage (population 195,756), located in the Pacific region of the United States

Characters:
Mr. Ronald Gates, Chief Marketing Officer
Ms. Christine Nicholson, Chief Executive Officer
(both of Carthage Mobility)
Mr. Buddy Ferguson, Television and Radio Personality

Context:
In this case, top executives of a personal mobility company debate how to proceed with marketing efforts after learning of their celebrity endorser's untimely death.

Christine Nicholson, Chief Executive Officer, and Ronald Gates, Chief Marketing Officer, both of Carthage Mobility, are at a loss for words. The two have just learned that Buddy Ferguson, a famous television and radio personality who was recently hired as the company's celebrity pitchman and just completed a series of production shoots for several personal mobility advertisements, was killed in an automobile accident. This is devastating to the two executives for a number of reasons, not the least of which is the loss of someone that Christine and Ronald had enjoyed getting to know over the course of his work with Carthage Mobility. Beyond the personal loss, however, was that of the company's loss, and the fact that this occurred so recently after wrapping production of forthcoming marketing communications just makes matters worse.

Carthage Mobility recently gambled its entire marketing budget on Buddy's famous face, voice, and general appeal to target audiences and now that plan is in complete disarray. Struggling over their personal and professional loss, Christine and Ronald are working toward determining what steps the company can take to salvage their investment and anticipated prosperity resulting from Carthage Mobility's association with Buddy.

Carthage Mobility is a medium-sized manufacturer and distributor of personal mobility products, with its primary offering being powered chairs that permit those with physical limitations to have better access to the world around them. These chairs, which come in a variety of models, allow users to engage in activities, such as grocery shopping and general recreation, that would otherwise be impossible or, at the least, very difficult for given individuals. The company competes nationally and has become somewhat of a familiar name among those who are knowledgeable of personal mobility products, taking its place among five or six prominent companies.

Carthage Mobility takes marketing very seriously. Although Ronald formally was responsible for the Carthage Mobility's marketing efforts, Christine took an active role, as she herself was a former marketing executive. The two executives, in fact, graduated from the same university class, with both majoring in marketing.

Historically, Carthage Mobility followed the lead of many other personal mobility companies by extensively engaging in television advertising and direct mail campaigns. Its various marketing communications generally have focused on the quality of the company's products and the excellence of its service and support that is provided on behalf of its customers. Carthage Mobility's excellent products, coupled with excellent marketing communications, have afforded the company a solid piece of the market and associated prosperity, but in detailed discussions several months ago, Christine and Ronald indicated that they wanted more.

By their estimation, most mobility companies, including Carthage Mobility, were engaging in very similar communicative approaches using almost identical creativity. Christine and Ronald believed that if Carthage Mobility moved against the norm, taking a different approach, perhaps it would garner greater attention and ultimately permit the company to grab a larger share of the market. The two debated several options, ultimately determining that the hiring of a well-known personality had the potential to elevate the status and stature of Carthage Mobility.

After contacting several agents, Christine and Ronald realized that celebrities certainly do not come cheap. Even with extra cash infusions, hiring a celebrity will really burden Carthage Mobility. But in the end, the two executives considered this new but expensive pursuit to be an investment in the company and proceeded to search for a suitable celebrity to represent their product offerings.

As their product offerings primarily pertain to senior citizens, Christine and Ronald sought to identify a celebrity who had meaning to older populations. Additionally, the individual needed to possess a reputation that inspired confidence and trust. The celebrity's actual use of personal mobility products would be a definite bonus.

Of several celebrities who came to mind, Buddy Ferguson stood out. The 67-year-old had a distinguished movie and music career extending over 5 decades. He possessed broad-based appeal to many audiences, starring in movies of myriad genres, from action to comedy. His music career was always secondary to his life on the big screen, but he was successful nonetheless, primarily working with the country music format.

Buddy was no stranger to promoting products. He served as spokesperson for several companies, including an airline and a hotel chain, but was engaged in nothing that would conflict with Carthage Mobility's personal mobility product line. Further, it was learned that Buddy actually used personal mobility products on a limited basis for periodic assistance when an old injury, resulting from a fall off of a horse, flared up. All things considered, he was the perfect celebrity for the job. After negotiations with Buddy's agent, a deal was struck and he was scheduled to become the celebrity face of Carthage Mobility.

Christine and Ronald scheduled a production window and booked a crew to shoot what ultimately would become three versions of Carthage Mobility's new television advertising campaign featuring Buddy. The two executives were most impressed by Buddy's very personal nature, presenting himself more as a local friend than a Hollywood regular. Buddy indeed was a natural and proved to be the perfect pitchman for Carthage Mobility's product line. With everyone satisfied with the effort, production wrapped and a national television campaign was immediately booked. The advertisements were scheduled to run on a continuity schedule over the course of 1 year, primarily placed during morning and late evening hours, which the company found to contain viewers meeting desired demographics.

Everything was ready to go. In just 2 weeks, the national campaign would be initiated. All of Carthage Mobility's employees, especially Christine and Ronald, were very excited. Yes, Carthage Mobility indeed had spent a small fortune on the campaign—Buddy's fees, production costs, advertising media expenditures, and so on—but it was believed that the investment would pay massive dividends.

Everyone's sense of excitement came crashing to a halt, however, when it was learned that Buddy was killed in an automobile accident. According to live news reports, Buddy was returning home with his wife after the two had lunch at a popular Hollywood eatery, when their automobile was struck by a tractor trailer that apparently encountered some sort of mechanical failure. Both Buddy and his wife died instantly.

Being such a well-known figure, Buddy's death devastated the nation, generating condolences from far and wide. While Christine and Ronald, together with all other employees of Carthage Mobility, mourned the loss of a legend, the two executives wondered what steps to take regarding their advertising campaign. Buddy had already been paid, as had the production crew that shot the commercials. If the advertisements do not run, the expensive investment simply would turn into a massive loss. But if the advertisements do run, the public might find them to be outright offensive, or at least distasteful. The two recalled a number of campaigns featuring deceased celebrities, but the given celebrities had been dead for years, and, at least in some cases, used special effects to bring them back to life to pitch modern day product offerings; circumstances that were very different from the one involving Buddy. Christine and Ronald feel as though they are between a rock and a hard place and do not know what direction to take.

DISCUSSION

1. At the conclusion of the case, Christine and Ronald find themselves in a quandary. Carthage Mobility has spent a small fortune on an advertising campaign featuring, Buddy Ferguson, a celebrity, but before the advertisements even run, Buddy dies. Place yourself in the position of the two executives. Identify every possible course of action that comes to mind and discuss the pros and cons associated with each. What would you do in this situation and why?

2. Occasionally, companies air television commercials featuring deceased celebrities. Do any come to mind? If so, identify them. Generally speaking, what are your thoughts on advertisements featuring recently deceased individuals? What about individuals who have been dead for quite some time?

3. Assume that Christine and Ronald decide that Carthage Mobility has no other choice than to run the television advertisements featuring Buddy. Assume further that the advertisements feature Buddy commenting on the benefits of the company's product line and acknowledging that he looks to Carthage Mobility for his associated needs. How might such advertisements be modified creatively to make the best of a grim situation?

4. Aside from the use of a celebrity like Buddy, how might Carthage Mobility have generated equally prominent attention without the downside risk of death or perhaps impropriety on the part of human actors and actresses?

5. Although the case does not present specifics regarding Buddy's contract with Carthage Mobility, given the disaster, how might Christine and Ronald approach Buddy's agent to discuss payment matters? What are the possibilities?

29

Tit-for-Tat

SNAPSHOT

Institutions:
New Albany Hospital, a 315-bed, not-for-profit provider of general medical and surgical services
Highland Colony Medical Center, a 450-bed, not-for-profit provider of general medical and surgical services

Location:
New Albany (population 153,296), located in the South Atlantic region of the United States

Characters:
Mr. Melvin Dawson, Chief Marketing Officer
Ms. Tara Hearne, Chief Executive Officer
(both of New Albany Hospital)

Context:
In this case, a medical center's top marketing executive looks to grow market share but his strategies and tactics are matched at every turn by the market leader, effectively neutralizing his efforts.

Melvin Dawson, Chief Marketing Officer at New Albany Hospital, is perplexed. Despite his best efforts, in his 18-month tenure as marketing chief, he has been unable to gain any market share on behalf of his institution. It seems that every time Melvin experiments with a unique method to capture market share, the prime competitor and market leader in the region copies his given move, effectively neutralizing any potential benefit for New Albany Hospital. In the end, all of his efforts are proving to not only be fruitless, but also expensive, given that no return on investment is being recouped. Perhaps the only benefactors, in Melvin's estimation, are the various media companies and other firms benefiting from the increased marketing communications of the healthcare industry. The marketing communications mimicry has resulted in a market share draw, with the shares of New Albany Hospital and its chief rival not budging. Given this, Melvin is wondering what, if anything, can be done to elevate the status and stature of New Albany Hospital in the marketplace.

One and a half years ago, Melvin was hired to serve as New Albany Hospital's Chief Marketing Officer. Melvin was no stranger to marketing, having served for over 2 decades in the area, with the majority of his experience being in the healthcare industry. However, this was Melvin's first opportunity to serve as the top marketing executive of an establishment and he was very excited to do so. While most of his prior experience was gained in institutions that were defined market leaders with very limited competition, his new opportunity at New Albany Hospital placed him in a very different position, namely that of being in the second place position, behind a very savvy and powerful rival.

Based in New Albany (population 153,296), a city located in the South Atlantic region of the United States, New Albany Hospital has occupied the runner-up position in the region for over 30 years, falling far short of rival Highland Colony Medical Center in the battle for market share. After several decades of coming up short in the race for market leadership, New Albany Hospital's management and governing board seemed to be content with the institution merely holding its own against its powerful foe. However, the newly hired Melvin had his sights set on greater glory and had intentions to at least begin to challenge Highland Colony Medical Center, perhaps gaining a bit of share here and there. This, he believed, would keep New Albany Hospital's competitive skills honed. He also believed that any market share increases likely would improve morale and potentially serve as a springboard for greater gains. With the endorsement of the medical center's Chief Executive Officer, Tara Hearne, Melvin went about designing a marketing plan and associated strategies and tactics to ignite the competitive fire of the institution.

Having long accepted its runner-up position, New Albany Hospital did not heavily engage in marketing communications. The institution provided high-quality care and relied on the word-of-mouth referrals of satisfied patients for the bulk of its business. Melvin believed that the historic scarcity of marketing communications presented an opportunity, as the general public had not had much exposure to promotions messages of the institution over the years. This perhaps would help to jump-start the drive for growth.

In his investigation of the marketing communications used by Highland Colony Medical Center, the bulk of volume seemed to be directed toward billboard advertising. It seemed that, at least at present and in recent memory, television advertising was not utilized. Given this, Melvin believed that television advertising might very well be the pathway for building visibility in the marketplace, as this would be unique to New Albany Hospital. Of course, Highland Colony Medical Center could turn to television advertising as a response to New Albany Hospital's use, but Melvin anticipated that there would be delays in doing this, first to build the communications into Highland Colony Medical Center's promotions schedule and second to produce the television advertisement and book the airtime. This, in Melvin's estimation, would give New Albany Hospital valuable time to make an impression on audiences well before Highland Colony Medical Center pounced, if that even occurred. The key was to keep the production of New Albany Hospital's television advertising campaign top secret so as to delay competitive reactions for as long as possible.

With his mind made up and with the approval of Tara to initiate the television advertising campaign, Melvin worked with an advertising agency to develop the given advertisement and book the air time. He intentionally kept as many people out of the loop as possible to preserve secrecy and it appeared that his hard work paid off as on the day that the advertisements hit, countless employees indicated that they were very surprised to see and hear New Albany Hospital's television messages. Melvin was pleased with the end result and believed that this could very well put an end to the hospital's market share growth stagnation.

Melvin's feeling of exuberance, however, did not last long. In fact, it did not last through the week, as Highland Colony Medical Center began running television advertisements just 3 days after New Albany Hospital began to do so. Melvin was dumbfounded because he anticipated that a competitive response would take time to assemble and book, but the leverage of the market's leading healthcare entity was more intense than he had ever imagined. To make matters worse, the production value of Highland Colony Medical Center's television advertising campaign was clearly of higher quality than New Albany Hospital's, with Melvin assuming that the advertisements had been prepared in recent months as insurance against competitive threats, being ready for deployment if necessary. New Albany Hospital's foray into television advertising prompted the response. On further analysis, Melvin noticed that Highland Colony Medical Center's media purchases were far more numerous than those of New Albany Hospital. Essentially, New Albany Hospital was being pummeled by Highland Colony Medical Center on the television advertising front.

New Albany Hospital did not have the resources to up the ante. Its television advertising campaign ran its course, yet, adding insult to injury, Highland Colony Medical Center continued its television campaign for some time afterwards before it, too, ceased. Clearly, Highland Colony Medical Center was using a tit-for-tat approach in which the market leader copies the move of a weaker competitor, using its strength to ultimately block competitive moves and intents.

Feeling defeated, Melvin resigned himself to the fact that New Albany Hospital would need a new approach to gain market share and that it probably would require a cutting edge angle, perhaps some sort of unique differentiator that would be difficult for Highland Colony Medical Center to copy. What that would be, though, remained elusive, with Melvin realizing that intensive thought would be required to come up with an approach.

While he worked toward devising a unique solution that could not be easily replicated, Melvin decided that, minimally, New Albany Hospital should run billboard advertisements consistently in the marketplace, as Highland Colony Medical Center tended to rely on the medium. At least, New Albany Hospital would have a presence in the communicative landscape of the city.

At the beginning of the following month, New Albany Hospital's modest billboard campaign was initiated. All seemed well, until a few weeks later when, on his drive into work, Melvin noticed that Highland Colony Medical Center had, in fact, increased its number of billboard advertisements in the community, likely as a competitive response to New Albany's use of the medium. Melvin feels as though he should just give up.

DISCUSSION

1. It appears that Highland Colony Medical Center is engaging in the tit-for-tat strategy, copying the moves of the weaker opponent, New Albany Hospital. This strategy presents a serious dilemma for the runner-up entity trying to gain market share as every move taken essentially is blocked by the more powerful rival. What, if anything, can Melvin do to break this cycle and gain market share for New Albany Hospital?

2. Melvin indicated that after he realized that Highland Colony Medical Center was copying New Albany Hospital's actions, one possibility for gaining market share would be to do something that Highland Colony Medical Center would find difficult to copy. What might that be?

3. Although this case dealt with Melvin's perspectives as Chief Marketing Officer of New Albany Hospital, Highland Colony Medical Center clearly was deploying a bold defensive strategy. What are your thoughts on its approach to shutting down New Albany Hospital's efforts to gain market share? If you were the top marketing officer of Highland Colony Medical Center, would you have done anything differently? Why or why not?

4. A secondary point of the case pertained to Melvin's desire to keep New Albany Hospital's television campaign a secret until it was released. He was fortunate enough to pull this off, yet he still was outsmarted by Highland Colony Medical Center. Regardless, what could have happened had news of New Albany Hospital's upcoming campaign been leaked to Highland Colony Medical Center?

5. Think of the parties, both internal and external, who are involved in the development and production of advertising campaigns and the varying degrees of control you would have over them as a top marketing officer. How would you go about diminishing the likelihood of leaks which might tip off competitors of looming campaigns? How would you address internal versus external parties?

PART FIVE

Consumer Behavior and Target Marketing

Winning Over Customers

SNAPSHOT

Institution:
Boardwalk Clinic, a three-physician medical practice specializing in family medicine

Location:
Chelsea (population 279,044), located in the West South Central region of the United States

Characters:
Dr. Barbara Hayes, Co-Owner and Physician
Dr. Michelle Lewis, Co-Owner and Physician
Dr. Mark Montgomery, Co-Owner and Physician
(all of Boardwalk Clinic)

Context:
In this case, three physician–owners of a clinic experience success but are frustrated by the clinic's inability to retain patients, leading to an investigation of associated causes.

Dr. Barbara Hayes is stumped. After a few years of practice at various hospitals, she and two physicians from her medical school's graduating class decided to venture into the entrepreneurial world by opening their own clinic. By all accounts, their establishment, Boardwalk Clinic, is a success, but 24 months into the venture, Barbara is noticing a pattern that is somewhat troubling. Patient retention is very weak. Specifically, the clinic is witnessing a hardy volume of patients, making it economically viable, but repeat business is not as frequent as desired, weakening the clinic's position in the market.

In Barbara's mind, she and her colleagues are doing everything possible to accommodate patients, delivering the best available care with very personal service, leading her to believe that repeat business should be especially robust. But something apparently is missing. Perhaps elements of Boardwalk Clinic's business plan and marketing strategy are amiss. Knowing the importance of patient retention to the long-term success of healthcare establishments, Barbara sets her sights on getting to the bottom of this apparent problem.

Drs. Barbara Hayes, Michelle Lewis, and Mark Montgomery founded Boardwalk Clinic 2 years ago, filling a need in Chelsea, a city of 279,044 located in the West South Central region of the United States, for a private medical clinic that offered its services during both traditional and nontraditional hours. The clinic operates from 7 AM to 8 PM, 7 days per week, far exceeding the hours of operation of any of its competitors.

While the three physicians believed that operations during traditional hours would yield a viable patient population, they were especially enthusiastic about potential patient volume during nontraditional hours, given the lack of competitive options available and increasing demand for after-hours services stemming from the rise of dual-career couples and working single parents in and around Chelsea who often could not attend to medical wants and needs during regular business hours. Ultimately, they envisioned brisk patient volume.

Barbara and her colleagues took great pains to design a servicescape that would be most accommodating to their patients. For example, they ensured that parking was readily available and accessible, that the waiting room area was comfortable and appealing, that patient wait times to see practitioners were very minimal, and that care provided from admission to discharge was excellent. Further, employees, both clinical and administrative, were trained to deliver superior customer service and to improvise, addressing patient needs before the patients themselves even realized such.

The three physicians were true believers in following leading edge techniques for ensuring that their product offerings continually meet and exceed the wants and needs of patients. While they assembled medical service offerings in the manner they viewed to be best, they were always quick to consult consumers for their insights and opinions. For example, prior to Boardwalk Clinic's grand opening, the physicians test marketed the operation by offering a group of 12 Chelsea residents free physical examinations in exchange for their insights and opinions regarding Boardwalk Clinic's decor and accommodations, processes and procedures, care delivery, and customer service. They also initiated an ongoing patient satisfaction survey. Importantly, findings were acted on, ensuring ongoing attention to patient wants and needs.

Now 2 years into the venture, Boardwalk Clinic clearly has witnessed success. Patient traffic is high, especially during the evening and weekend hours, and the results of patient satisfaction surveys indicate that the vast majority of patients are very satisfied with the care provided by the clinic. This gave Barbara and her colleagues a great sense of accomplishment in knowing that they largely were meeting and exceeding the expectations of their patients. But in the area of patient retention, the clinic is not meeting their expectations, dampening their overall sense of accomplishment and defusing what would otherwise be considered to be a total entrepreneurial victory.

Seeking answers to the patient retention issue, Barbara decided to conduct an intensive investigation. Over a couple of weeks, she intensively reviewed patient records, satisfaction surveys, and related documents in an effort to shed light on Boardwalk Clinic's inability to witness robust repeat patient business. Her findings were insightful but unfortunately yielded no smoking gun.

Specifically, Barbara observed that during traditional hours of operation—Monday to Friday from 8 AM to 5 PM—Boardwalk Clinic appears to be developing a loyal patient base, with many choosing to return for medical services after their first visit, something somewhat expected as surveys indicated that many of these patients did not have a current family physician. However, Barbara discovered that during nontraditional hours of operation—early mornings, evenings, and weekends—the clinic is struggling to convert first-time visitors into loyal customers. As the bulk of Boardwalk Clinic's patient volume occurs during nontraditional hours, Barbara considered it to be especially unfortunate that patient retention is weakest during this period.

Seeking more detail, Barbara decided to probe deeper, interviewing patients presenting during nontraditional hours over the course of several days, asking them about their future medical patronage plans. Through these interviews, she learned that the vast majority of patients visiting Boardwalk Clinic during its non-traditional hours of operation planned to return to their current medical providers, using Boardwalk Clinic only during times when their current caregivers were unavailable. Thus, patients presenting during nontraditional hours of operation most often select Boardwalk Clinic not as their first choice, but as their only choice, just for those odd times that their current providers cannot be seen. On the positive side, a number of patients interviewed by Barbara indicated that they planned to select Boardwalk Clinic as their medical provider of choice. Unfortunately, of all interviews conducted, this was the minority view, making Barbara uncertain as to whether she and her colleagues could wrestle loyal patients away from their established relationships with competing providers and clinics.

Barbara knows the difficulties associated with acquiring patients who are loyal to their current providers and now understands that Boardwalk Clinic, by offering extensive hours beyond any other provider in the community, will continue to see a great deal of first-time/only-time patients. But she also knows that conversion of patients from first-timers into loyal customers is a key to survival, growth, and prosperity.

With a better understanding of the retention matter, Barbara now realizes that she and her colleagues must direct their attention toward shoring up loyalty from patient traffic experienced during nontraditional hours of operation. Having established leading edge services throughout Boardwalk Clinic, Barbara currently is at a loss as to what steps her clinic can take to entice those patients in the Chelsea marketplace who already have relationships with other medical entities to make Boardwalk Clinic their medical provider of choice. She has scheduled a meeting with Drs. Lewis and Montgomery to discuss her findings and brainstorm about possible courses of action.

DISCUSSION

1. From the information supplied in the case, it is very apparent that Boardwalk Clinic operates in a manner that is attentive to the wants and needs of its customers and is very focused on the market. In your own words, define the term "market orientation" and itemize the elements noted in the case that illustrate Boardwalk Clinic's deep commitment to this particular orientation.

2. Barbara's investigation indicates that Boardwalk Clinic indeed is accumulating loyal patients, particularly those presenting during traditional business hours, but retention is weak in patient populations presenting during nontraditional business hours, especially in cases where patients already have established medical relationships elsewhere. Should poor retention here be of concern? Why do you believe this to be the case?

3. Barbara indicated that she is stumped when it comes to improving patient retention among first-time/only-time patients who already have established medical relationships and are visiting Boardwalk Clinic only due to immediate needs occurring when current providers are unavailable. What might Barbara and her colleagues do to influence these patients to make Boardwalk Clinic their medical provider of choice? List at least five things that would serve to entice patients to return.

4. Using a consumer behavior or similar marketing textbook as a guide, for each enticement that you noted in Inquiry 3, scientifically describe how the given enticement is expected to impact patients. In preparing your descriptions, reflect on consumer psychology and various models of consumer decision making as you go about shedding light on each enticement's anticipated consumer impact.

5. Continuing your investigation of consumer behavior and psychology, identify several models that are capable of explaining why Boardwalk Clinic is having difficulties attracting patients who are loyal to other medical care providers. How might the insights gained from these models provide assistance to Barbara and her colleagues or any other person seeking to attract satisfied patrons from competitors?

31

Teasing with Price

SNAPSHOT

Institution:
Ashford-Collins Dental Clinic, a recently established provider of dental services

Location:
Newport (population 1,552,259), located in the West South Central region of the United States

Characters:
Dr. Thomas Ashford, Co-Owner and Dentist
Dr. Russell Collins, Co-Owner and Dentist
(both of Ashford-Collins Dental Clinic)

Context:
In this case, two entrepreneurs establish a dental clinic but despite intensive efforts, they cannot seem to attract a viable patient population, leading them to contemplate the use of teaser pricing in their marketing communications.

Drs. Thomas Ashford and Russell Collins, co-owners of Ashford-Collins Dental Clinic, have their backs up against the wall. They recently established their dental practice, but after many months of hard work, they have achieved very little traction in the market. Despite their best efforts, patient volume remains low and the lack of a sustainable patient base, much less growth, is forcing them to reconsider their marketing strategies and tactics. They must find a solution to bolster their poor patient volume very quickly or they will have no other choice than to close their dental practice.

Ashford-Collins Dental Clinic was established 1 year ago by Drs. Ashford and Collins, following their retirement from the armed services where they served as dentists for military servicemen and women. Together, they possess over 40 years of dental experience; however, they are new to entrepreneurship, making this endeavor especially challenging. Drs. Ashford and Collins did not haphazardly decide to enter private practice; they had been planning to do so for years. Stationed together through much of their military careers, the two sought to craft career pathways following their military service and believed that private practice would be a prudent course of action. In preparations for this, they enrolled in business courses, occasionally attended entrepreneurship seminars, and studied their intended marketplace, which happened to be the city where they both were born and raised—Newport.

Newport (population 1,552,259), is a thriving metropolis located in the West South Central region of the United States. As one would imagine, the teeming population of the city requires a robust supply of dental practitioners to address the associated healthcare wants and needs of Newport's many residents. Newport indeed has a thriving dental health complex, with dental offices being located seemingly on every corner. This, however, did not deter Drs. Ashford and Collins because they believed that even with market saturation, their dental practice could capture patients through excellent patient care and attention, together with savvy business strategies and tactics.

Shortly after leaving the military, the dentists began putting their plan into action. Using personal savings and loan assistance from a Newport bank, the two secured equipment, furnishing, and an office suite at a retail center located in the prosperous Northside Hills section of the city. The specific location of their suite offered excellent roadway visibility because it was situated just off of a main traffic corridor, something that facilitated access as well. Parking was excellent and neighboring businesses offered complementary healthcare services, including a retail pharmacy, medical clinic, wellness center, and vision center.

Drs. Ashford and Collins appointed their clinic in an aesthetically pleasing and comfortable manner, taking great care to think of patient wants and needs. Pleasing color combinations, comfortable waiting room and examination chairs, an audio system that piped soothing music throughout the facility, and a wealth of customer service-oriented staff members represented just a few of the many things that the two dentists incorporated to provide an outstanding patient experience.

The two dentists test marketed their clinic prior to its official grand opening by inviting a few of their friends over to have complimentary dental examinations in exchange for their thoughts regarding the clinic and its associated level of service. This information proved invaluable as it directly influenced them to alter several aspects of the clinic, including the layout of the waiting room, further enhancing and enriching the patient experience.

With their dental services in good order, Drs. Ashford and Collins knew that the next step would be to communicate their service offerings to the public appropriately, with the intention of stimulating interest, attention, and ultimately patronage. In their investigations of marketing communications options, they were stunned at the expense of some media types. Television advertising on the major networks proved to be catastrophically expensive, given the high-profile market and expansive population of the city that the local television stations served. The same was true of display advertising in Newport's two newspapers. But that did not deter Drs. Ashford and Collins, as on further investigation, they believed these media involved too much wasted circulation, delivering messages across the city and beyond. They envisioned their market to be in fairly close proximity to their dental practice, primarily drawing on consumer and business clients located within a 7-mile radius of the clinic.

Radio was a possibility, but the dentists believed that they would be required to purchase air time on too many stations to reach desired target markets, a necessity resulting from massive audience fragmentation caused by dozens of stations catering to many listening tastes and preferences. Multiple station purchases elevated costs to points considered prohibitive. Wasted circulation was again a problem noted by the two, forcing them to opt against using the medium.

Billboards, however, seemed to be a good choice to Drs. Ashford and Collins because of the high reach and frequency they generate in comparison to other mass media, especially when costs are considered. Further, billboards could be purchased in desired geographic areas, limiting the incidence of wasted circulation.

In addition to billboards, the dentists turned to other communicative methods, namely direct mail marketing, personal selling, and public relations. Through direct mail, homes and businesses within the designated market area of the dental practice were targeted precisely. Further, the dentists targeted area businesses using personal selling, where the clinic's office manager periodically visited area establishments, speaking with owners and employees about the dental practice and leaving behind promotional brochures. Public relations rounded out the mix, with Drs. Ashford and Collins ensuring that press releases were prepared and submitted to media outlets whenever newsworthy events occurred, such as the clinic's grand opening, the provision of a new dental service, or the hiring of a new employee.

With this particular communicative mix, Drs. Ashford and Collins believed that they could effectively convey their service offerings to their target audiences, but after several months of deployment, it was apparent that the mix was not working. Patient volume was merely a trickle. Satisfied that their dental offerings were on the mark, evidenced by both test marketing and customer feedback, they blamed the poor results on a failure to communicate with target audiences.

As budgetary limitations prohibited the deployment of additional communicative resources, the dentists were pressed to find a communications pathway that would actually drive patronage. In working toward resolving their dilemma, Drs. Ashford and Collins began discussing the use of teaser pricing as a means of attracting value-minded customers, hoping to convert them into regular patients. Perhaps they could run a deal-of-the-month for various dental procedures, such as teeth cleaning or teeth whitening services. The deal could be placed on billboards and in direct mail flyers, communications devices that were already in use. And to give the impression of enhanced value, the practice could use odd (e.g., $99.95, $399, etc.), as opposed to even (e.g., $100, $400, etc.), pricing in promotional messages.

Drs. Ashford and Collins believed that deals at rates that were priced 15% to 25% lower than equivalent offerings in the market would provide powerful provider-switching incentives to patients in Newport. Given the economical pricing, the two dentists envisioned perhaps that their patient draw might be extended to areas beyond the 7-mile radius that they initially targeted.

Although this clearly is not the path that Drs. Ashford and Collins intended to pursue, they feel pressured to do something, especially as the very viability of their practice is at stake. Inexperienced in the art and science of entrepreneurship and facing dwindling resources, the two dentists continue their discussion and debate over whether to turn to teaser pricing in an attempt to generate patronage.

DISCUSSION

1. Drs. Ashford and Collins initially designed, to the best of their ability, a marketing communications mix that they believed would be capable of reaching their target audiences. Prepare a critical review of their selections and associated rationale, indicating any gaps noted and how you would go about closing them.

2. The two dentists appeared to discount the obvious saturation of dental practices in Newport, believing that they could capture patronage by providing an enhanced level of service and attention. Does this perspective demonstrate the naivete of the dentists? Why or why not?

3. Feeling the pressure of lackluster patient volume, Drs. Ashford and Collins consider using teaser pricing to promote Ashford-Collins Dental Clinic. What are the promises and pitfalls of resorting to such a tactic? What would you anticipate the consumer response to be? Do you think this will save Ashford-Collins Dental Clinic?

4. Although the case presents limited information, based on what you have learned both in the case and in your marketing studies, what other strategies and tactics might Drs. Ashford and Collins turn to besides teaser pricing to increase patronage?

5. Although Drs. Ashford and Collins blame the poor patient volume of their clinic on a failure to communicate with target audiences, what other factors might be leading to their misfortune? For each factor that you identify, what course of action would you take to eliminate the given obstacle and bolster patient volume?

Stopping Outshopping

Timothy Rogers, President and Chief Executive Officer of Scarlet Hospital, has a dilemma. His institution is facing an interesting and potentially threatening situation which ironically is the result of something beneficial occurring in the community. Specifically, an interstate highway is being extended from Salem, a large metropolitan area of 187,452 residents, to

Walnut Grove, a small community of 25,454 residents located approximately 50 miles away, which serves as the home of Scarlet Hospital.

This new transit route, located in the Mountain region of the United States, will reduce the travel time between Salem and Walnut Grove from just over 1 hour via a winding two-lane local highway to approximately 40 minutes via the modern four-lane interstate highway, dramatically improving the accessibility between the two cities and beyond. While this development has the potential to yield many benefits for Walnut Grove, it also will usher in a new set of challenges to every business in the city, as Walnut Grove will become less distant—at least in terms of travel time—to the larger city of Salem and its burgeoning pool of competitors eager to attract new business from outer-lying communities. Needless to say, this has Timothy concerned, knowing that Scarlet Hospital will face challenges associated with retaining its patient population, given improved access to Salem and its four major medical centers.

Timothy has served in his current position at Scarlet Hospital for the past 14 years and he has witnessed many challenges over that time period. Dealing with competition, however, has not been much of an issue in recent years, making the threat associated with the new interstate an especially challenging matter. A 350-bed, not-for-profit medical care provider, Scarlet Hospital is the only hospital in Walnut Grove, the result of a merger between two competing hospitals over a decade ago, and is the largest healthcare provider within a 50-mile radius. The distance between Scarlet Hospital and the larger metropolitan areas teeming with healthcare institutions has benefited the facility in that consumers in the marketplace historically have been inclined to look to Scarlet Hospital for delivery of healthcare services, viewing more distant facilities simply to be out of reach.

In fact, the only competition in the marketplace has been in the area of outpatient care, as Walnut Grove is the home of several medical practices that compete with Scarlet Hospital on several service fronts. All in all, Scarlet Hospital has enjoyed delivering medical services in a highly insulated market, softening its competitive prowess, but not its commitment to quality, thanks to Timothy's philosophy of delivering the highest quality medical care possible.

Whereas some institutions would use this isolation to provide second-rate services, taking advantage of the captive market, Timothy has always believed in delivering the best and striving to outdo past efforts at every opportunity. He, too, demands this commitment from all employees.

For this reason, Scarlet Hospital has maintained standards of excellence in care delivery that rival those of institutions in much larger cities, giving him confidence that the hospital will be able to compete in the quickly approaching, more competitive environment.

When the highway extension was announced 1 year ago, Timothy called a meeting with Scarlet Hospital's senior management team and outlined the situation, stating that the team would need to devise a defensive plan for deployment no later than 6 months in advance of the opening of the highway. He also advised everyone to keep a watchful eye on the marketplace, reporting any indication of competitive activity immediately. He noted that, just as in any market, some outshopping will occur, with patients looking to external markets for institutions to address their healthcare wants and needs, but that the increased accessibility to Salem would likely hasten such. Their job, Timothy insisted, was to ensure that outshopping did not become epidemic.

Timothy's points were well taken by all. Scarlet Hospital's senior managers each knew the risks of doing nothing as many hospitals in smaller cities over the years have watched their patient bases dwindle at the hands of more aggressive competitors in larger cities, effectively skimming given communities of their most valuable and profitable patients. Those patients with few or no resources are left, as they simply do not have the means to look to other markets for healthcare services. As a result, cost shifting opportunities become more limited, with threatened financial viability and closure being worst case scenarios. The team dedicated themselves to ensuring that this did not occur.

At the 6-month point, Scarlet Hospital's senior management team had developed a defensive plan that primarily increased the hospital's advertising efforts, securing more billboards than it had in previous years, introducing radio advertisements for the first time in many years, and bolstering other forms of marketing communication. Scarlet Hospital was fortunate in that its commitment to quality over the years meant that the physical plant, clinical and administrative staff members, and quality of care rendered all were top notch, meaning that upgrades, other than those that naturally occur within any progressive entity, were not necessary to gain parity with larger institutions. The team felt confident that their actions would protect Scarlet Hospital's market share and the plan was immediately initiated.

Three months prior to the opening of the highway, Timothy and his staff members began noticing local advertisements—mostly billboard and newspaper ads, and a few radio spots—promoting healthcare institutions in Salem. Much as they anticipated, Salem's healthcare institutions viewed Walnut Grove's population as a source of growth, given upcoming improvements in accessibility. The advertisements generally stressed that Salem would soon be within easy reach of Walnut Grove. That was troubling enough to Timothy and his senior managers, but perhaps the most disturbing aspect pertained to overtones in the advertisements that health care delivered in the "big city" is better.

Timothy's greatest concern was that the advertisements were creating the perception that care is perhaps less effective at Scarlet Hospital. Given this, it was very clear that Scarlet Hospital, whose advertisements served primarily as reminders of the excellent quality and care delivered by the hospital, would need to be more aggressive in its marketing communications, as it was apparent that the battlefront would be one of perception. Waging war on this front would no doubt require intensive planning, something Timothy vowed to initiate immediately in an effort to address the most significant threat that Scarlet Hospital has witnessed in many years.

DISCUSSION

1. Courtesy of Timothy's philosophy of continually striving for excellence, Scarlet Hospital was well prepared to compete with establishments in Salem even before the highway improvements mandated such. What lessons does this case teach healthcare executives about never becoming complacent, despite being in environments that might permit such luxuries?

2. It appears that the healthcare institutions in Salem are making strong moves to attract patients from Walnut Grove, threatening Scarlet Hospital. Timothy indicated that, given the competitive advertisements' suggestions that "big city" medicine is better, the battlefront will be one of perception. What do you believe he meant by this statement?

3. Timothy notes that the nature of competitive advertisements placed by Salem-based healthcare institutions in Walnut Grove calls for Scarlet Hospital to be more aggressive in its marketing communications efforts. Based on your knowledge of marketing and the information supplied in the case, how would you go about addressing these advertisements and why would you take such steps?

4. The case provides a reasonable amount of detail regarding Scarlet Hospital's defensive plans. Based on your knowledge of marketing and the information supplied in the case, provide a critical review of Scarlet Hospital's defensive plan. If you were an employee of Scarlet Hospital and Timothy asked you how you would go about shoring up the plan, what would you suggest and why?

5. Although the case provides limited information, it seems that Timothy is completely discounting a potentially very positive outcome resulting from the new interstate highway, namely that it might provide a chance for Scarlet Hospital to attract patients from the Salem marketplace. Outshopping, therefore, might be a real concern for healthcare establishments in both Walnut Grove and Salem. Timothy outlined his defensive strategy, but did not address an offensive one. Think deeply on the possibilities, given the scenario provided in the case, and formulate an offensive strategy that could be deployed by Scarlet Hospital to turn the tables on Salem-based healthcare providers.

A Few Degrees Off Target

SNAPSHOT

Institutions:
Willow Hills, a 75-unit assisted-living property planned for construction over the forthcoming 12-month period
Willow Properties, a multiproperty, for-profit provider of assisted-living services

Location:
Belmont (population 377,392), located in the Mountain region of the United States

Characters:
Ms. Jennifer Kennedy, Management Trainee
Mr. Samuel Stevens, President and Chief Executive Officer
(both of Willow Properties)

Context:
In this case, a management trainee is tasked with completing an independent target marketing exercise for a soon-to-be-constructed assisted-living property, but despite good reviews by corporate leaders, her plan still needs work.

Jennifer Kennedy, Management Trainee at Willow Properties, is stressed. One month ago, she was issued her first big challenge. Having worked intensively for several weeks, she now has completed the assignment and is scheduled to meet with corporate leaders to present her findings. The pressure is on as she knows that her performance will impact her future career path at Willow Properties.

Jennifer was asked to engage in a target marketing exercise for Willow Hills, a 75-unit assisted-living center that will be built over the next 12 months, with its grand opening following shortly thereafter. Willow Hills is located in the city of Belmont (population 377,392), which is situated in the Mountain region of the United States. It will become the 19th assisted-living center owned and operated by Willow Properties.

Located approximately 75 miles from the corporate office, Willow Hills represents the first Willow Properties' operation in Belmont, a city teeming with long-term care services, but one worthy of entry given its reputation as a highly desirable retirement community. Still, it represents a new market that Willow Properties must gain familiarity with in order to attract occupants to Willow Hills.

Specifically, Jennifer was assigned the responsibility of segmenting the market and selecting target populations, upon which marketing communications then would be developed in an effort to attract the patronage of the defined audiences. This was a big assignment for her, especially given her relative inexperience. At the time of her assignment, she only had 6 months of professional employment experience, having accepted the Willow Properties opportunity just after earning her Bachelor of Business Administration from a local university.

Ordinarily, such an extensive assignment would not be placed on the shoulders of a management trainee, but Willow Properties operates a somewhat unique management training program that emphasizes experiential learning, as opposed to simple observation. The training program is the brainchild of its President and Chief Executive Officer, Samuel Stevens. An educator at heart, Samuel is an advocate of learning by doing; that is, actually having trainees engage in the activities required of experienced managers. He believes that by placing trainees in roles that actually require independent thinking, a better manager emerges.

Samuel and his executive team members are known for providing comprehensive guidance at the onset of major assignments, but then withdrawing that assistance at opportune moments, forcing the trainees to make independent decisions. In addition to fostering independent thought, judgment, and accountability, this approach also tests each trainee's ability to address the unknown and perform under stress. This helps corporate leaders to identify those who eventually will assume the executive ranks at Willow Properties, ensuring proper succession planning in the growing corporation.

On meeting with executive team members, Jennifer was given a thorough overview of the target marketing assignment, the expectations held by the leadership of Willow Properties, and the timeline for completion. Case studies of several assisted-living centers owned by Willow Properties also were presented to enlighten her. With the assignment formally conveyed and the motivation of knowing what was at stake, Jennifer got to work immediately on her task to segment the market of Belmont and its surrounding vicinity appropriately and target desired segments of the population.

Beginning her work, Jennifer first consulted a marketing textbook for guidance, specifically locating a table of segmentation variables that presented sample groupings based on geographic, demographic, behavioral, and other characteristics of populations. Calling on this to assist her in identifying potential market segments, she then crossed each of the potential segments with the product at hand—assisted-living services—and examined each of the resulting combinations seeking to identify appealing segments that would have wants or needs for Willow Hills' services and the means to extend patronage. Jennifer knew that she would be required to factor in wealth, because the population would need to be able to afford Willow Hills' expensive lease rates, and geographic region, as she envisioned that Willow Hills would primarily serve the residents of Belmont who were desirous of assisted-living services.

Based on her investigation, Jennifer believed that the ideal target market for Willow Hills would be the senior population (60 years of age and older), possessing sufficient financial resources ($100,000+ annual income or equivalent resource access), and residing in or near the city of Belmont (within a 30-mile radius of the Willow Hills' property). She based her opinion on several factors, including the fact that seniors were the actual users of assisted-living services, that sizeable financial resources would be required of these individuals in order for them to pay the lease amount over a sustained period of time, and that the physical location of the assisted-living center would likely attract those who resided locally.

In reaching this target audience, Jennifer selected a pathway that she viewed to be obvious. Specifically, she believed that Willow Properties would do well to place Willow Hills' advertisements in media that attracted senior audiences. Consulting several advertising sales representatives in Belmont, she devised a sample campaign that involved the use of television, radio, and magazine advertising. Advertisements would run only during television shows that appealed to senior audiences, on radio stations running music formats that appealed primarily to older audiences, and in magazines that specifically focused on senior health and wellness initiatives.

Jennifer, feeling as though she had thoroughly addressed her target marketing assignment, formally prepared her report and scheduled its presentation with the leadership of Willow Properties. On presentation day, Jennifer meticulously presented the task requirements, her associated methodology, and her findings and recommendations.

At the conclusion of her presentation, Jennifer was asked to leave the conference room for a brief moment, permitting Willow Properties' executives to privately assess her efforts before giving her formal feedback. While waiting outside of the conference room, Jennifer's heart raced as she replayed her presentation over and over again in her head, hoping that she had addressed the target marketing assignment properly. After what seemed like an eternity, she was asked to return to the conference room for feedback.

On returning for formal feedback, much to Jennifer's relief, Samuel, speaking on behalf of his fellow executives, expressed appreciation for her efforts and indicated that she made some very valid points. He further expressed that for someone who had never conducted a target marketing assessment, he was very impressed with her work. However, Samuel did indicate that there were deficiencies that she would need to address, but he noted that these are to be expected of anyone engaged in a learning experience.

When Jennifer asked for insights regarding the nature of her plan's deficiencies, Samuel, seeing value in withholding some insights to force management trainees to dig deeper, gave her a simple hint, stating that her assessment was incomplete. He asked her to think on this and return in 1 week with a revised plan.

Relieved on one hand, stressed on the other, Jennifer left the conference room, challenged to make sense of Samuel's modest feedback and craft a revision to her target marketing plan for Willow Hills. Much work remains.

DISCUSSION

1. At the conclusion of the case, Samuel noted that he was impressed with Jennifer's work, but challenged her to think deeper, indicating that her efforts at target marketing were incomplete. Although the case does not provide a definitive answer, what do you believe Samuel was suggesting to Jennifer? What did she overlook or omit in her analysis on behalf of Willow Hills?

2. Although the case provides some indications of associated requirements, investigate the process of target marketing and prepare a step-by-step practitioner guide that could be used to carry out this activity. Select a local community with which you are familiar and, using the product of assisted-living services, demonstrate how you would go about using this guide.

3. What is your opinion of the experiential learning process embraced by the leadership of Willow Properties? Do you believe, as Willow Properties' corporate executives do, that this particular type of learning process yields more capable management professionals than observation-based learning processes? Why or why not?

4. Assume that Jennifer was correct in her identification of Willow Hills' target market. What is your assessment of her associated marketing communications proposal? Do you believe the marketing communications vehicles that she selected were appropriate and complete, given her target audience? What changes, if any, would you suggest?

5. If you were in Jennifer's position, how would you go about deciphering Samuel's hint that her findings were incomplete? She obviously had put much into the analysis, but still came up short. With only 1 week to prepare a revised report, what actions might she take in order to gain insights that would close gaps and completely impress the leadership of Willow Properties?

34

Take It or Leave It

SNAPSHOT

Institution:
Scott County Medical Clinic, a five-physician medical practice specializing in family medicine

Location:
Centerville (population 1873), located in the South Atlantic region of the United States

Characters:
Ms. Erica Davis, Administrator
Dr. Bill Ferguson, Managing Partner and Physician
(both of Scott County Medical Clinic)

Context:
In this case, the longtime administrator of a rural clinic seeks to better accommodate the wants and needs of its patient population but learns that the establishment's physician–owners see no reason to do so because of complete market dominance.

Erica Davis, longtime Administrator of Scott County Medical Clinic, cannot believe it. For the 15th time this week, a patient has called asking for an evening appointment at the clinic. This trend began several months ago and appears to be intensifying. Unfortunately, however, Erica must inform patients that the clinic cannot accommodate their requests because it does not hold extended hours. Callers are then informed of the clinic's 8 AM to 5 PM, Monday through Friday schedule after which they typically go ahead and schedule appointments accordingly.

Erica honestly wishes that she could say that patients continue their appointment bookings because of their loyalty to Scott County Medical Clinic, but she knows the real reason. Patients in the marketplace have no convenient option for medical treatment at any place other than Scott County Medical Clinic because the five-physician practice is the only medical clinic in a 40-mile radius of Centerville. In other words, patients either alter their personal schedules to accommodate the clinic's hours of operation or face the prospects of an 80-mile round trip to another medical provider, something few residents in the area can afford to do.

As suggested by its name, Centerville serves as the center of a very isolated rural market in the South Atlantic region of the United States. The city of Centerville has a population of just 1873 residents, but it is surrounded by scores of tiny communities each of which look to Centerville for various goods and services, as the hub of the region.

Clearly, Scott County Medical Clinic is situated in a market of captive patients. Even the prospect of intermarket competition is slim because the rural area simply does not have enough patient volume to attract another medical practice. Despite the low population, however, Scott County Medical Clinic is bustling, as it draws not only on the population of Centerville, but also on the surrounding small towns. With no competition, the clinic is economically viable.

Erica is not particularly well educated—she acquired most of her skills via on-the-job training, taking the position of Administrator shortly after graduating from a local community college where she earned an Associate of Arts in Business Administration—but she worked diligently to understand Scott County Medical Clinic's customers. Although untrained in marketing research techniques, she had the wherewithal to maintain a log of unmet wants and needs, a product of her commitment to customer service.

This simple log permitted her to track points of dissatisfaction that she worked diligently to address and ideally remedy. In the past, she had discovered and remedied problems with the interior signage in the clinic, increasing the size of the text to better accommodate those patients with poor vision; patient transportation, partnering with a local taxi service to give economical rates to Scott County Medical Clinic's patients; and admissions expediency, installing a software program that improved associated efficiency and effectiveness. Now she has targeted the evening hours issue and is committed to resolving that as well.

Seeking background information pertaining to her latest customer service concern, Erica began asking patients desirous of evening appointments about their associated motivations for the late appointments. Most patients responded that their employment obligations did not allow them the luxury of taking off during business hours to attend to their medical concerns. This made perfect sense to Erica. She was well aware that the community was home primarily to employees earning hourly wages, making absences from work costly, because they would not be paid. She also had taken note that the largest employer in the area, a farm equipment manufacturing plant, had recently increased production adding more employees to the day shift, giving further credence to patient responses.

While Erica's log permitted her to notice the spike in requests for evening appointments and her very basic research gave indications of its cause, coming up with a resolution is proving to be problematic. Earlier in the month she approached the managing partner of the clinic, Dr. Bill Ferguson, asking if she could have a moment of his time to discuss her customer service concerns. Dr. Ferguson agreed.

In the ensuing meeting, Erica communicated that she was noticing an increasing number of requests for evening appointments. She had done her homework and instead of sharing anecdotal information with Dr. Ferguson, she shared facts, presenting the number of requests for late appointments, as well as the dates and times of desired appointments.

Knowing that it is always best to supply a solution whenever a given problem is noted, Erica suggested that Scott County Medical Clinic consider extending its hours of operation to accommodate these requests. She also noted that the number of requests for late appointments would likely increase further given the nature of the workforce and the status of associated workforce operations in the area. She even prepared a grid estimating the patient volume anticipated during a possible 5 PM to 7 PM evening hours schedule, noting that it would be economically viable and might even help to resolve the periodic overcrowding that is occasionally experienced during Scott County Medical Clinic's normal business hours. Presenting supporting information gained from patients, Erica asked Dr. Ferguson if Scott County Medical Clinic could make associated accommodations.

Dr. Ferguson was very appreciative of Erica's hard work at coming up with a solution to a problem she was noticing and very much was impressed by her concern for patients in the Centerville area. However, he communicated that he was not motivated to make any changes. His rationale was based on the fact that Scott County Medical Clinic did not have any competition. Given this, Dr. Ferguson believed that the clinic was not in danger of losing any of its patients, leading him to question why the clinic would even consider making any scheduling changes. On top of this, he noted that neither he nor his physician colleagues had any interest in working extended hours, preferring to maintain current operating practices. Dr. Ferguson thanked Erica for her work, but quickly dashed her hopes that Scott County Medical Clinic would take action to better accommodate the patient population of the region.

Since her meeting with Dr. Ferguson, Erica has struggled to make sense of things. While she well understands the benefits of having a captive audience, she knows that those benefits must be respected; otherwise, complacency results, often leading its unsuspecting victims right into its jaws of destruction. Further, from her business courses at the local community college, she knew that a take-it-or-leave-it attitude was a formula for disaster. Even in a small town like Centerville, who is to say that a competitor cannot or will not enter the market and siphon off business from complacent establishments?

Sitting in her office, Erica looked upon Scott County Medical Clinic's mission statement, prominently displayed on her wall. One phrase in particular stood out, "Scott County Medical Clinic will strive to continuously meet and exceed the wants and needs of its patients." She had helped create this mission statement years ago and, by and large, the clinic followed its tenets. But it appears now that customer wants and needs were addressed only when it did not inconvenience the clinic's owners.

Erica understands that extended operations would indeed carry inconveniences for Scott County Medical Clinic's owners and employees and that logistical challenges would also result, but she believes such hardships would give way to better customer service, rewarding everyone in the long run. Leaving work at the end of the day, she thought to herself that a solution had to exist—one that would suit both the clinic's owners and its patients. She vowed to find an answer.

DISCUSSION

1. Thinking of the evolution of marketing, and its noted eras of development, which era would best characterize the mindset expressed by Dr. Ferguson and his physician colleagues at Scott County Medical Clinic? How does this philosophy go against modern marketing thought?

2. At the conclusion of the case, Erica expresses concerns regarding the future viability of Scott County Medical Clinic, noting that it seemed to be violating a basic tenet stipulated in its mission statement associated with striving to meet and exceed the wants and needs of its patients. Assume that Scott County Medical Clinic continues on its given course and fails to offer extended hours of operation. What are the possible consequences?

3. Erica vows to find a solution that will bring Scott County Medical Clinic back into compliance with its mission statement, noting that there had to be a way to accommodate the wants and needs of both the clinic's owners and its patients. What options would you suggest and why?

4. Assume that Scott County Medical Clinic suddenly learns that a competitor is entering Centerville. Do you think this would motivate Dr. Ferguson and his physician colleagues to consider extending the hours of operation of the clinic? Why or why not?

5. In this case, Scott County Medical Clinic is clearly the market leader in Centerville, albeit resulting from the total absence of competitors, something that Dr. Ferguson expects to continue. Regardless of the unique circumstances of Scott County Medical Clinic, this case has many implications for any market leader, regardless of the particular marketplace of operation or quantity of competitors faced. Think deeply on the case and your knowledge of marketing and identify and discuss the lessons that it can provide for any market leader.

35

Through Others' Eyes

SNAPSHOT

Institution:
The Bo Sutton Foundation, a not-for-profit establishment focusing on the promotion of healthy habits, behaviors, and lifestyles to the teenage population

Location:
Corinth (population 217,377), located in the West South Central region of the United States

Characters:
Ms. Greta Sutton, Founder and Administrator, The Bo Sutton Foundation
Mr. Rod Young, Account Executive, Desert Plains Media

Context:
In this case, the head of a healthy practices foundation targeting teenagers makes the mistake of believing that her establishment's target audience sees the world as she does.

Greta Sutton, Founder and Administrator of The Bo Sutton Foundation, considers herself to be informed—now, at least. She just committed a major gaffe when she made the assumption that her establishment's target audience viewed the world and its various stimuli just as she does. While she knew and knows that this is not the case, she found herself falling into this common trap as she went about making decisions regarding a promotional campaign for The Bo Sutton Foundation. Specifically, she based elements of the campaign on her personal perspectives rather than on those of the population that the given campaign targeted.

In the end, the campaign was a resounding failure, costing the foundation precious resources. Despite the failure, on the positive side of things, Greta has gained a better understanding of target marketing and consumer behavior, specifically, and marketing, generally. Given this, she is destined to make better decisions in the future by reminding herself of the intricacies of human perception and the associated impacts of demographic factors on such. But it took quite a tumble for this to register with her.

Greta founded The Bo Sutton Foundation after experiencing a very tragic and traumatic event. Three years ago, her teenage son, Bo, died in an automobile accident. The loss of her son was a bad enough event to experience but to make matters worse, he was driving under the influence of alcohol, making his death entirely his own fault. Fortunately, no one else was injured by his negligence. Bo was in a one-vehicle accident without any passengers. Intoxicated, his car traveled off of the roadway and directly into a roadside tree. He was killed instantly.

Greta was a single mother, working as a business executive in an effort to provide the best she possibly could for Bo, her only child. Her work as an executive required long and late hours at the office, as well as frequent overnight travel, giving her little time to spend with Bo. Still, she believed that she was doing the right thing in that she was able to do more for her son and for herself than would be possible otherwise. At every possible turn, she endeavored to educate Bo, encouraging him to make good decisions in order to avoid negative consequences, but she knew that he occasionally got carried away and made poor decisions, as many teenagers do. Still, it never occurred to her that tragedy was near at hand.

Late one Friday night, after a high school football game, she heard a knock at her door. Thinking perhaps that Bo had lost his key, she answered the door but instead of seeing her son, she was greeted by two police officers who conveyed that Bo had been involved in an automobile accident and died at the scene. Although test results were in process, the officers conveyed that it was very apparent through evidence found at the scene of the accident that he had been consuming alcohol. This was further confirmed by high school students who were with Bo just before the accident.

In one simple moment, Greta's world was turned upside down. Between tears of sadness and fond remembrances, Greta could not help but blame herself for Bo's death. She tortured herself with thoughts that if she had been more involved in his life and less involved in her work that this would never have happened. She was left with no one and nothing. Her life descended into utter chaos.

Then, months later, she began to regain control of her life. Through her network of friends and coworkers, coupled with spiritual counseling, she began to pull herself back up from the grimmest of places in life. She embarked on a personal quest to work toward ending, or at least minimizing, the potentially destructive behaviors of teenagers. Greta decided that the most appropriate tribute to her son, as well as therapy for herself, would be to start a foundation focused on the promotion of healthy habits, behaviors, and lifestyles, specifically targeting the teenage population. The foundation would encourage teenagers to refrain from the use of alcohol and tobacco products and avoid other high-risk behaviors, with abstinence being the major push. She named the foundation after her son to honor his memory.

Based in her hometown of Corinth, a city of 217,377 residents located in the West South Central region of the United States, The Bo Sutton Foundation was funded by resources that were previously earmarked by Greta for Bo's university studies, along with federal grant monies provided to entities seeking to promote healthy lifestyles. With resources in hand, Greta went about implementing a very detailed plan for communicating the dangers of unhealthy practices to teenagers. Her primary mechanism for delivering this information involved simple, but highly effective presentations in which she would meet with student groups, recount the tragedy that took her son's life, discuss how and why the tragedy occurred, convey the sense of pain and grief that she felt in the aftermath of the tragedy, and encourage members of given audiences to make better decisions. Her message was very powerful and seemed to impact audiences, sometimes bringing some teenagers to the point of shedding tears on hearing of Greta's trials and tribulations.

As time went on, Greta sought to reach more audiences and knew that she, as a sole speaker, had limitations in the number of teenagers she could reach. She decided to turn to mass media for assistance. Specifically, she sought to fund a television advertising campaign that would convey the dangers of alcohol abuse, generally, and underage consumption of alcohol, specifically. She envisioned that the advertising campaign would first target the population of Corinth and the surrounding vicinity and then move to other areas of the region and perhaps eventually be aired across the nation.

Greta was very satisfied with her idea and the timing could not have been better, because the high school football season would be beginning soon. Given that many parties occur afterwards and the fact that her son died as a result of consuming alcohol at one such party, Greta believed that this would make for an excellent time to run the foundation's advertisements, hopefully preventing some teenagers from making poor decisions. Because Greta was unfamiliar with marketing communications, never having served in any marketing capacity in her executive career, she decided to turn the project over to Rod Young, an account executive at Desert Plains Media.

Meeting with Rod to discuss creativity and communication desirables, Greta conveyed the mission of The Bo Sutton Foundation, the target audience, and necessities for reaching teenagers effectively. With Greta's information, Rod returned to Desert Plains Media and began the process of assembling a creative vision that would meet Greta's desirables.

Two weeks later, Rod invited Greta to Desert Plains Media to review a storyboard for the foundation's proposed television advertisements. There, Greta met the creative team that had worked on the storyboard. It consisted of a series of eight panels, with written and visual descriptions of the occurrences tied to each of the panels. Rod indicated that the campaign would feature a series of six commercials, with the first five all ending with a "to be continued" wrap-up, to keep viewers interested and on the edge. The advertisements centered on "Shelley," a teenage girl who is faced with a series of dilemmas frequenting the teenage population, forcing her to make choices along the way. The first advertisement introduces Shelley and sets the stage for subsequent commercials in which she faces choices regarding with whom she should socialize, what to do when alcohol is being consumed by everyone and peer pressure to join in reaches a fever pitch, and similar issues. The final advertisement throws a wrench into the fray, with viewers being led to believe that Shelley will make the right choice, but instead she makes the wrong one and loses her life at the hands of her poor decision.

Greta was deeply impacted by the intensity of the campaign and its shocking conclusion, which would not be revealed until the fourth month of the campaign. The message was powerful and the "to be continued" feature kept attention and interest high. While she also viewed the advertising theme to be personally upsetting as it was an open reminder of the loss of her son, she believed the impact of the message would be needed to bring teenagers to their senses. Without hesitation, Greta decided to green-light the project, turning over production to the skilled personnel at Desert Plains Media.

Over the next couple of weeks, Desert Plains Media produced the series of advertisements with free reign as Greta assigned all creative decisions to the agency. When production wrapped, editing took place with the final campaign being completed and ready for distribution 1 week later. Greta was invited back to Desert Plains Media to view the product of the team's hard work. As the first advertisement was played, Greta was shocked. The advertisement featured a club scene with blaring, annoying music and flashing lights. Further, the girl cast as Shelley was dressed entirely inappropriately, looking, from Greta's perspective, more like a prostitute than a high school student. At the conclusion of the advertisement, Greta indicated that she would never allow such a poorly composed campaign to run and demanded that changes be made immediately.

Rod and his staff at Desert Plains Media worked to convince Greta that the creative elements and approach were extensively tested with teenage focus groups and proved to be high impact. They also indicated that the scenario and atmosphere presented in the advertisements were accurate depictions of social scenes that teenagers actually encounter and experience. The look of Shelley, too, was an accurate portrayal of how teenage girls routinely dress. Greta was unconvinced and demanded that the advertisements be redone. This time, she would be involved in the creative process and in production.

Several weeks pass and, with Greta's input, the production of the campaign finally wrapped, with the end result being a very toned down series of advertisements featuring the same storyline, but with very different, highly conservative visual and auditory elements. The campaign was initiated—and it immediately flopped. Subsequent research indicated that the campaign was viewed very favorably by the adult population, particularly those who were middle-aged or older, but the teenage audience viewed the advertisements very negatively; they simply could not relate to what they viewed to be very outdated images, out of touch music, and overall lameness.

Greta's eyes were opened wide, as she learned firsthand of the perils of failing to see things through the eyes of target audiences. In essence, she formulated a campaign that appealed to her, not to the target audience. It proved to be a fatal error.

Rod requested permission to run the original campaign formulated by Desert Plains Media. Greta authorized the campaign and it was a success.

Greta learned a valuable lesson regarding target marketing and consumer behavior. She also now has a profound knowledge and awareness of the costs associated with making marketing mistakes.

DISCUSSION

1. Greta clearly was upset with the initial series of advertisements created by Desert Plains Media. Although Greta turned all aspects of creativity over to Rod and his advertising agency, do you believe that Rod should have kept Greta informed of decisions that were made throughout the process to ensure her satisfaction? Who was ultimately to blame for the miscommunication and misunderstanding between client and agency?

2. Greta immediately vetoed the initial campaign produced by Desert Plains Media, yet she had no experience in the area of marketing communications. Given this, do you believe Greta should have trusted those with expertise in the area, at least giving the campaign a chance to work, before changing all of its creative elements? Why or why not?

3. In this case, Greta makes the fatal error of designing a promotional campaign that suited her tastes and preferences rather than those of her foundation's target audience. Unfortunately, such a mistake is not very uncommon, as, even though executives typically know better, they are drawn into the trap of seeing things through their own eyes, rather than the eyes of others. Why do you believe that this error occurs?

4. In an effort to avoid falling into the trap, as did Greta, of viewing promotional campaigns through one's own eyes, what mechanisms might you put into place to remind yourself to look through the eyes of target audiences when designing promotional campaigns?

5. Assume that you have an understanding that you should look through the eyes of target audiences when designing promotional campaigns. How would you go about actually gaining insights from designated target audiences regarding given creative ideas and advertising messages?

The Scorned Customer

SNAPSHOT

Institution:
Westlake Medical Center, a 515-bed, not-for-profit provider of general medical and surgical services

Location:
Kent (population 344,572), located in the West North Central region of the United States

Characters:
Ms. Patti Bronson, Vice President of Marketing
Mr. Victor Martinez, President and Chief Executive Officer
Ms. Lisa Reed, Staff Nurse
(all of Westlake Medical Center)
Mr. Brian Jenkins, Freelance Graphic Artist and Web site Designer
(son of Dorothy Jenkins)
Ms. Dorothy Jenkins, Homemaker (former patient of Westlake Medical Center, now deceased)

Context:
In this case, a medical center faces the wrath of a patient's family member who chooses a unique way to lash out at the establishment.

Patti Bronson, Vice President of Marketing at Westlake Medical Center, is very concerned. It seems that Brian Jenkins, the son of a former patient, Dorothy Jenkins, who recently lost her battle with cancer at the medical center, has taken anger and frustration to an entirely new level. A freelance graphic artist and Web site designer, Brian has developed an anti-Westlake Medical Center Web site, alleging inferior treatment delivered by the establishment, and has secured several domain names that are very similar to the one held by Westlake Medical Center. The end result is that many of the medical center's patrons are inadvertently directed to the rogue Web site where they are greeted by accounts of poor treatment and inferior customer service at Westlake Medical Center. Patti has dealt with disgruntled patients and their families in the past, but this is a very new situation in that, unlike word-of-mouth transferred from person to person, the rogue Web site has the potential to reach massive audiences, openly broadcasting negative allegations. Patti knows that Westlake Medical Center must respond to this threat, but she is uncertain as to which particular approach to take.

This all started 6 months ago, when Dorothy presented in Westlake Medical Center's emergency department with chronic pain. She was admitted in a timely manner and given the best care possible, but the fact of the matter was that she was in the advanced stages of pancreatic cancer and there was nothing that Westlake Medical Center, or any other healthcare entity, could do except provide her with as comfortable a life as possible for the remaining weeks of her life. Westlake Medical Center did just that and, by every account, Dorothy was very accepting of her fate and indicated her sincere appreciation for the care and treatment delivered by the medical center. She died 3 months after her initial presentation at Westlake Medical Center's emergency department.

Life went on at the Kent-based, 515-bed, not-for-profit establishment, and it was assumed that, for Dorothy's family, the same was true. But shortly after Dorothy's death, her son, Brian, began writing letters to the medical center's governing board members claiming that Westlake Medical Center failed his mother, alleging that more could and should have been done to save her life. The governing board did, on occasion, hear from disgruntled patients and occasionally was forced to contend with lawsuits. The matter essentially remained unaddressed and unacknowledged by the governing board, because it was believed that in such cases, little could be said or done, especially with the knowledge that the given patient did, in fact, receive the best possible care that Westlake Medical Center could provide. Following standard practice, the correspondence was turned over to legal counsel to ensure that the institution was protected.

As the weeks passed, Brian was not heard from and it was assumed that he perhaps had come to terms with his mother's death. However, it soon came to light that, instead of consulting an attorney for the purpose of suing Westlake Medical Center, Brian used his skills as a graphic artist and Web site designer to lash out at the medical center. This was brought to Patti's attention by a staff nurse, Lisa Reed, whose friend happened to come upon Brian's rogue Web site while searching for Westlake Medical Center using a popular search engine. Westlake Medical Center's Web site was listed first in the search listings, but immediately after the official listing was Brian's rogue Web site. Lisa informed Patti that her friend clicked on the link to Brian's Web site and witnessed its profound dedication to disparaging the institution on every imaginable front, advising patients not to seek care at Westlake Medical Center. On learning of this, Lisa believed that Patti needed to know immediately and advised her accordingly.

Patti immediately informed Victor Martinez, Westlake Medical Center's President and Chief Executive Officer, and began her own investigation, as this particular Web site threatened the identity of the establishment and had the potential to do very real harm by deterring patients from directing their patronage toward the medical center. She performed the same search that Lisa's friend conducted and, just as indicated, Westlake Medical Center's Web site, followed by the rogue Web site, appeared.

The first thing that entered Patti's mind was that the potential for confusion was very high in that the rogue Web site's domain name, www.westlakemedicalcenter.net, aside from its suffix, was identical to Westlake Medical Center's official Web site address, www.westlakemedicalcenter.com. On further review, Patti discovered that Brian had also secured the .org and .info suffixes for "westlakemedicalcenter," creating the potential for even more confusion. Further searches revealed that several anti-Westlake Medical Center domain names, including www.westlakekills.com and www.westlakemedicalcenterkills.com, were also secured, all directing visitors to the rogue Web site. This was a very well-planned effort.

In reviewing the contents of the rogue Web site, Patti noticed that its primary feature centered on a report, authored by Brian, detailing missed opportunities by Westlake Medical Center and its caregivers to save Dorothy Jenkins' life. Brian clearly indicates that he is the designer of the Web site, stating that he felt the need to warn others of the potential harm and even death that can result by entrusting Westlake Medical Center to deliver care. Among other things, the Web site included a "Top 10" list of reasons not to present for care at Westlake Medical Center, various accounts from other citizens who claim to have experienced inferior care and treatment at the medical center, and a list of things that concerned citizens can do to ensure that Westlake Medical Center alters its practices to be a better servant of the community, with directing care delivery to other institutions being the leading method for initiating change at the facility.

With this information, Patti met with members of the care delivery team that attended to Dorothy as a check to ensure that Westlake Medical Center indeed provided the leading care and attention that has been a mainstay at the establishment for decades. The caregivers confirmed that they followed standard protocols for care and treatment, but they also acknowledged that Dorothy's son, Brian, was constantly problematic, questioning their judgment and decision making without any basis for doing so. He was not difficult to the point of requiring assistance, instead, the caregivers simply had to tolerate a constant stream of inquiries, with Brian often commenting that he read about techniques on the Internet that were said to deliver better results than the techniques being used by the medical center.

As Brian was not the responsible party and Dorothy was deemed to be fully capable of guiding her medical care and treatment, the caregivers did their best to appease Brian, but they were more concerned with doing their best to assist Dorothy. Brian's interference, in their eyes, simply boiled down to a family member who was having difficulties coping with the inevitable.

With Patti fully convinced that Westlake Medical Center did its part responsibly and professionally, she began to think about the marketing ramifications of the rogue Web site. Questions of how to stop it began to enter her mind, as did concerns over what might come next. These questions and others no doubt will be addressed when she meets with Westlake Medical Center's executive team and legal counsel this afternoon as the establishment seeks to address the latest crisis.

DISCUSSION

1. In this case, Westlake Medical Center faced the wrath of a patient's family member who claimed mistreatment when the facts, and even the comments made by the patient in the final weeks of her life, indicated otherwise. This resulted in the family member designing a rogue Web site that sought to discredit Westlake Medical Center. Think of the options available to Westlake Medical Center in this situation and list each of them. Feel free to use external sources to compile your options list.

2. Of the options presented in Inquiry 1, which one would you choose and why?

3. It appears that Westlake Medical Center did nothing to deserve the punishment being inflicted by Brian and his rogue Web site. However, what if the medical center indeed had played a role in Dorothy's demise. Would this situation cause you to change the particular option selected in Inquiry 2? Why or why not?

4. Westlake Medical Center apparently had not secured multiple domain names that were similar to the one that actually was used by the establishment. This gave Brian the opportunity to secure very similar domain names that gave his deviant plan added impact. Should Westlake Medical Center have been more proactive in protecting its online identity? Please justify your response.

5. In an ideal world, Brian's Web site would never have been constructed because his concerns would have been addressed to his satisfaction by Westlake Medical Center. This may or may not have been possible, even with great efforts directed accordingly by the medical center, as Brian might not have responded positively to reasonable explanations. Regardless, what steps can healthcare establishments take to ensure that disgruntled customers' concerns are addressed proactively, rather than immediately ushered off to legal counsel? Could Westlake Medical Center have done more to address Brian's concerns before he constructed the rogue Web site? What would you suggest, if anything?

PART SIX

Environmental Analysis and Competitive Assessment

37

Changing Times

SNAPSHOT

Institution:
Liberty Discount Drugs, an independent retail pharmacy

Location:
Avon (population 44,779), located in the East South Central region of the United States

Characters:
Ms. Laura Winters, Owner and Pharmacist
Mr. David Parker, Staff Pharmacist
(both of Liberty Discount Drugs)

Context:
In this case, the owner of an independent retail pharmacy is puzzled that store sales have plateaued but it takes the perspectives of an outsider to help her understand why.

Laura Winters is at a loss. Sales at her retail pharmacy are stagnant and have been so for quite some time. She is fortunate that she is maintaining her current level of business, but nothing seems to lift sales volumes. In recent months and years, Laura has attempted to revitalize her business and prompt growth, but her efforts have failed to generate traction in the marketplace. Knowing that stagnation ultimately leads to failure, she is determined more than ever to get to the bottom of things and has made this her top priority.

199

Laura is the owner of Liberty Discount Drugs where she also serves as its chief pharmacist. Liberty Discount Drugs is an independent retail pharmacy located in Avon, a city of 44,779 situated in the East South Central region of the United States. As for the competitive landscape in Avon, it is fairly stable, with the area not seeing the introduction of a new pharmacy in nearly 7 years. This starkly contrasts with a prior period in which Avon witnessed the arrival of a number of large national retail chain pharmacies, which placed pressure on the independent retail pharmacies in the market. This ultimately forced the closure of several independent pharmacies in Avon. Fortunately, however, Liberty Discount Drugs survived this tumultuous period and currently operates alongside several national chain stores and a few independent pharmacies in the city.

Laura became the owner of Liberty Discount Drugs 15 years ago, immediately after graduating from pharmacy school, but she has always been familiar with store operations. Liberty Discount Drugs was founded by her father 35 years prior to the transition of ownership. She essentially grew up at Liberty Discount Drugs and has never worked at any other place of business. This focused experience is a good thing on one hand, in that Laura has familiarity with the history and operations of Liberty Discount Drugs, but bad on the other, in that it has limited her exposure, something that is especially problematic in that this can lead to myopic perspectives of the marketplace and result in missed opportunities.

Liberty Discount Drugs' primary revenue generator rests with prescription pharmaceuticals, but critical secondary revenue comes from the store's moderately sized consumer goods and services retail section. This section, located in the front part of the store, includes everything from candy and detergent to digital film processing and package shipping services. In addition to the revenues generated by consumer products retailing, this component also serves to draw customers into the store, providing opportunities for Liberty Discount Drugs to capture their lucrative prescription pharmacy patronage.

With a 50-year history in Avon, Liberty Discount Drugs has its share of loyal customers, some spanning generations of the same family, creating a stable customer population, but the store has had difficulties in growing its customer base, causing sales to plateau. Market share has been level for quite a few years, this despite numerous attempts to push sales higher, including the renovation of Liberty Discount Drugs' retail space 5 years ago, improvements in parking 3 years ago, frequent placement of advertisements in local newspapers, use of direct mail solicitations sent to target markets, and the initiation of low-price guarantees on prescriptions. All of this, however, has served only to maintain, not grow, Liberty Discount Drugs' customer base.

Laura understands that her lack of experience at other pharmacies both within and outside of Avon probably is limiting her ability to break the sales stagnation that she has been witnessing. She simply has not experienced varying business scenarios and learned methods to adapt operations and overcome obstacles. Knowing this, Laura has come up with an idea that just happened to coincide with another business necessity—the hiring of a new pharmacist to replace one who was retiring.

Laura has already selected a candidate—David Parker—and forwarded an offer that David has accepted. David is an experienced pharmacist and, in previous employment positions, he also has managed business operations. He is seeking to move to Avon from a much larger metropolitan area, giving him fresh eyes in which to view and evaluate Liberty Discount Drugs and the city of Avon. David is scheduled to begin his new position of employment at the end of the month, but in the meantime, Laura asked him to study Liberty Discount Drugs in the context of the marketplace of Avon and surrounding communities and seek to identify methods to boost sales. David happily agreed to do so, promising to share his views when he reports to work.

A couple of weeks pass by and, on David's first day of work, the topic of sales growth is first and foremost in Laura's mind, with her eager to hear David's insights and suggestions. Happy to share his perspectives, David conveyed that, based on his informal market research over the past 14 days or so, he viewed Liberty Discount Drugs to be stuck in a time warp of sorts, noting that from his perspective, the drugstore had not changed with the times. He pointed out that the store indeed had been modernized over the years, that customer service was excellent, and that a loyal customer base exists, but Liberty Discount Drugs appeared to be addressing the populace of Avon as it was decades ago—a predominantly white community—rather than addressing the marketplace as it is today—a multicultural city with large populations of whites, blacks, and Hispanics. The demographic composition of the city and even the section of the community surrounding the store had changed over the years, spurred on by changing perspectives of society, the growth of industries in the area that created new jobs and fueled growth, and related matters.

David noted that after a review of consumer products on Liberty Discount Drugs' store shelves, he found nothing to indicate that the store was addressing the wants and needs of the multicultural marketplace. He noted that, as any consumer behavior text will confirm, tastes and preferences between and among different populations, at least in some cases, will be different, and that Liberty Discount Drugs was not addressing these differences. Although the consumer products retailing section of the store provided only a secondary revenue source, it was very important for the purpose of drawing customers' pharmaceutical business. Without providing consumer products that appealed to diverse audiences, the draw of this component of the store was unnecessarily limited.

Of equal concern, David observed that the advertisements and other marketing communications forwarded by Liberty Discount Drugs featured only members of the white population, potentially deterring minority patronage. Given everything he noted, it was very clear to David that Liberty Discount Drugs was ignoring the fastest growing populations in the marketplace. He believed that, with a redirection of attention to diverse audiences, the drugstore likely would witness increasing sales.

Laura's eyes were opened. While Liberty Discount Drugs had successfully attracted some patronage from minority populations in the area, business had never been as robust as she had desired. Acknowledging her limited exposure to other establishments and markets, it simply never occurred to Laura that Liberty Discount Drugs' product selection and advertising were serving as potential deterrents to patronage.

Through David's past exposure to many pharmacies and marketplaces, he was able to see something that had been elusive to Laura. With good effort and attention, Laura believed that sales from growing, diverse populations could give Liberty Discount Drugs the boost that it needs to move beyond the sales plateaus witnessed in recent years. With a newfound perspective of how to attack the problem of sales stagnation, Laura and David decided to work toward crafting and implementing an effective plan of action.

DISCUSSION

1. Based on your knowledge of this case and of the discipline of marketing, what errors of good marketing practice do you view Laura to have committed? How would you suggest that she rectify those errors and forge a path toward marketing excellence for Liberty Discount Drugs. Please justify your responses.

2. David indicated that the consumer products at Liberty Discount Drugs fail to adequately address the wants and needs of the multicultural marketplace. He notes that the store appears to be focused primarily on addressing the wants and needs of the white population and that this is a potential deterrent to minority customers. Based on the information provided in the case, what products or product variants might have been missing from the store shelves at Liberty Discount Drugs? You might wish to visit a large pharmacy in a diverse area of your local market to address this inquiry better.

3. David notes that the advertisements deployed by Liberty Discount Drugs lacked minority representation, citing this as a potential reason for the store's inability to attract minority customers. Do you believe advertisements that feature minority populations play a role in attracting the patronage of these groups and, if so, to what degree? Please justify your views on this matter.

4. Assume that you are planning to open an independent retail pharmacy in your local market. Give the hypothetical establishment a name and select a particular location in the market where the store will be situated. Then, estimate the store's trading area and analyze the population demographics in this area. Assuming that your store sought broad-based patronage from those in the trading area, design a newspaper advertisement promoting its grand opening that would broadly appeal to the populations surrounding the establishment. While a hand-drawn sketch will suffice, an advertisement designed using graphics software is preferred.

5. In this case, Laura has neglected to monitor the environment surrounding Liberty Discount Drugs and her establishment is paying the price for her oversights. Although the case presents an extreme example, oversights and failures associated with monitoring the environment are quite common. What steps would you recommend to ensure that institutions do not neglect the important duty of environmental surveillance?

Connecting the Dots

SNAPSHOT

Institutions:
Fairfield Drugstore, an independent retail pharmacy
Century Drug, a large national retail chain pharmacy, operating drugstores across America

Locations:
Madison (population 12,519), located in the Mountain region of the United States
Rockville (population 217,074), an urban area located 30 miles to the south of Madison

Character:
Mr. Patrick McDonald, Owner and Pharmacist, Fairfield Drugstore

Context:
In this case, the owner of an independent retail pharmacy credits his marketing surveillance system for giving him an advanced warning of a competitive threat.

Patrick McDonald, owner of Fairfield Drugstore, considers himself to be very lucky. He has always been a close observer of the market and it appears that once again his efforts have paid off—and this time they have really paid off big. Specifically, Patrick has learned that a new competitor, Century Drug, will be entering the market in less than 1 year. While he is not excited about the prospect of a new rival setting up shop in the community, Patrick is thrilled that through his surveillance activities he was able to uncover Century Drug's plans well in advance of a formal announcement. This will give him critical time to formulate competitive strategies and take defensive actions prior to Century Drug's grand opening.

Patrick founded Fairfield Drugstore 20 years ago to answer a critical need for a comprehensive retail pharmacy in the town of Madison, a small community with a current population of 12,519, situated on the outskirts of Rockville, a city of 217,074 in the Mountain region of the United States. Patrick noticed that the three retail pharmacies at the time, all of them being independent, focused primarily on pharmacy services, with consumer goods retailing being very limited. Through Fairfield Drugstore, Patrick introduced a thriving consumer goods component to complement his pharmacy business, differentiating his store from its competitors and better serving the wants and needs of residents, especially those who did not have regular access to Rockville, which was located half an hour away. Not only could customers get their prescriptions filled, they also could process their film, ship packages, have keys made, wire money, and purchase almost any consumer good that could be found in a traditional discount store, making Fairfield Drugstore a very well-rounded retail establishment.

As a result of Patrick's customer orientation, Fairfield Drugstore quickly became the market leader and has held that position in the community for years. Despite his success, Patrick has never become complacent and has continued to seek and incorporate innovations and improvements. He surveys customers and acts on the findings and periodically hires mystery shoppers to visit the store and report findings associated with their customer experiences. He also closely monitors the environment through planned marketing surveillance activities.

Patrick's particular marketing surveillance program involves daily monitoring of the local and state newspapers, permitting him to monitor, among other things, pharmacy advertisements as a means of ensuring that he offers consistently better deals to his customers. He also maintains memberships in local business and civic organizations and actively participates in associated meetings and events, permitting him to network with others. Further, Patrick holds memberships in various pharmacy societies and associations and regularly reads trade journals to stay abreast of the latest developments. To help him keep track of matters, he chronicles business developments on a whiteboard in his office, permitting important elements to remain at the forefront of his mind.

Patrick's drive to glean information from the marketplace permitted many of his prior successes and he has always found ways to capitalize on opportunities and defend Fairfield Drugstore against competitive threats. He was, for example, able to determine that a competing pharmacy in Madison was attempting to expand when he noticed an increasing number of employment advertisements for the pharmacy in the state and local newspapers, coupled with a tip-off provided by a fellow member of a civic organization. Further, noting the names of two Madison natives in a listing of honor students in his pharmacy school's newsletter, Patrick was able to recruit them as staff pharmacists, gaining commitments from each of them well in advance of the recruitment rush as candidates near graduation. In each of these examples and many more, Patrick was afforded with strategic advantages that otherwise would have been missed had he not kept his eye on the market.

So now Patrick's marketing surveillance activities have allowed him to identify perhaps the most beneficial marketplace intelligence of his career—Century Drug's upcoming entry into the Madison market—but addressing the threat will be another matter entirely. Ordinarily, one might expect to receive 5–6 months notification of such an entry, but thanks to Patrick's detective work, he has significantly increased the time he has to mount a defense. Patrick's discovery, once again, resulted from his efforts to connect the dots.

In fact, Patrick had been expecting new competitors to enter the market, given the changing environment in and around Madison. In recent years, Madison has witnessed increasing growth, courtesy of its proximity to Rockville and the metropolitan area's burgeoning population. This has resulted in overflow that has spread into Madison and beyond. Fairfield Drugstore has benefited from the increasing growth but Patrick well knew of its potential to attract competitors, possibly placing Madison in the crosshairs of large national retail chain pharmacies. Given the changes in the area, he became especially vigilant, looking for indicators in the community that suggested the introduction of new and different competitors.

Because he believed that large chains would not be interested in purchasing existing pharmacies that forced them into floor plans that would not meet their specifications, he anticipated that the purchase of vacant land would be required upon which a custom structure could be built. This led him to begin closely monitoring commercial property transactions in the local newspaper, being especially attentive to transactions involving companies unfamiliar to him. He also closely watched the state and local newspaper's classified advertisements seeking pharmacists for "new opportunities in growing communities" or something similarly generic in order to maintain as much secrecy as possible prior to expansion plans being formally announced. Additionally, in confidence, he asked his friends in real estate and economic development businesses in the town to keep him posted on any developments.

With his surveillance net cast far and wide, Patrick almost immediately witnessed the dots begin to connect, first hearing a rumor at a civic event, then seeing a Century Drug classified advertisement in one of the state's newspapers that promoted "exciting R.Ph. opportunities in several thriving locations." Posing as an interested applicant, Patrick contacted the advertisement's information hotline and asked if opportunities in Madison were going to be available. The response was that Century Drug was rapidly growing and that several locations, including Madison, certainly were possibilities. A land transaction fitting the bill also was revealed through Patrick's efforts, leading him to a holding company that, on further investigation, was discovered to be associated with Century Drug, confirming market entry in coming months.

Thanks to his efforts, Patrick now has valuable time to mount a defense, but he is very apprehensive. Never before has he had to compete against a large national retail chain pharmacy and he well knows that survival will be very challenging, given the strength of these establishments. Pausing only briefly to commend himself for discovering Century Drug's expansion plans, Patrick now must direct his attention to developing a plan to compete against his strongest competitor to date.

DISCUSSION

1. Patrick's marketing surveillance system that he implemented on behalf of Fairfield Drugstore was simple, yet surprisingly effective, indicating that massive resources are not necessarily required to build and maintain a productive marketing dashboard. He noted that he used a whiteboard upon which he posted the latest developments to help him keep matters at the forefront of his mind. Why might this method of presentation be better than listing developments in a notebook or even in a computer file?

2. The case presents a reasonable amount of information regarding Patrick's marketing surveillance system, but it does not go into intricate detail regarding the specific sources of information he called upon, civic clubs he joined, and so on. Assume that you are the owner of an independent retail pharmacy in your local marketplace. Design a marketing surveillance system that would permit you to stay abreast of the latest developments. Be sure to provide a detailed description of your system, identifying the sources of information you would call upon, methods of implementation, and related features.

3. Seeking competitive intelligence, Patrick posed as an interested applicant and called the information hotline that was listed in Century Drug's classified advertisement. In your opinion, was this ethical behavior? Why or why not?

4. Speaking of ethics in marketing surveillance, there are numerous methods for investigating people, places, and things, many of which can provide valuable information for business operations seeking to stay ahead of the competition. Think deeply on surveillance methods and list every technique that comes to mind. Are there things you simply would not do, regardless of the information that the given technique could provide? Why or why not?

5. At the conclusion of the case, Patrick indicates that he is very apprehensive, because Fairfield Drugstore, a small, independent retail pharmacy, will be facing a large national retail chain pharmacy in the coming months. Although the case does not provide insights as to how Fairfield Drugstore will compete with Century Drug, what techniques would you recommend? How might small establishments successfully compete against larger establishments?

Defining Competition

Drs. Christopher Cook and Paul Davidson are excited. They have made the decision to formally plot their departure from employment with a hospital-based cosmetic surgery practice and strike out on their own. They plan to establish a new clinic in a neighboring state which they plan to name Northside Cosmetic Surgery Center. In anticipation of this pursuit, the two physicians have been saving money for several years and, with further funding assistance from a local bank, they believe that they can make their dream become a reality. Although Drs. Cook and Davidson have informally sketched their vision for this endeavor, they never have formalized this vision—at least until now.

The two physicians learned that their lending institution requires a formal business plan as part of its assessment of business viability for the purpose of determining creditworthiness. As such, they must reduce their vision to writing, something they welcome as this plan also will be needed for very practical purposes—to ensure the efficient and effective operation of their proposed establishment.

Although Drs. Cook and Davidson lack formal training in business administration, they have attended several seminars on business planning and development and feel very confident that they can prepare an adequate and acceptable document that will meet the expectations of both the bank and themselves as future entrepreneurs. Among other things, the two have been asked to conduct a competitive assessment and, given their familiarity with the city that will soon be home to their cosmetic surgery clinic, they decided to address this component of their business plan first.

Drs. Cook and Davidson plan to base their clinic in Bristol, a city of 189,515 situated in the East North Central region of the United States. Both physicians were raised in Bristol, but after medical school they were drawn away to Kingston, a larger city in another state where they have been serving as cosmetic surgeons. Always envisioning a return to their place of birth, the two physicians stayed abreast of the cosmetic surgery marketplace in Bristol and believed that they likely could develop a competitive assessment from memory alone. Given what was at stake, however, they decided to formally explore and investigate the competitive landscape of the city to ensure accuracy in their assessment.

Bristol was selected as the future home of Northside Cosmetic Surgery Center for a number of reasons. First, Bristol is the hometown of Drs. Cook and Davidson, giving the city sentimental value. But they also view Bristol to be ideal in that the city is witnessing significant population growth, something projected to continue over the next decade. This, coupled with the overall increasing demand for cosmetic surgery services, makes Bristol the perfect home for the new clinic.

In initiating their competitive assessment, Drs. Cook and Davidson first consulted the Bristol telephone directory, as it provided a list of all of the cosmetic surgery centers that view the city's population to be a target market. This served as a check on their existing knowledge of competing centers in Bristol and helped to ensure that they did not inadvertently overlook any given cosmetic surgery establishment. Then Drs. Cook and Davidson plotted each establishment's location on a map permitting them an overall geographical view of the competitive landscape. By their count, Bristol was the home of seven freestanding cosmetic surgery centers, with an additional two practices being tied to medical centers in the city. Bristol was located approximately 50 miles away from any urban environment, making for a fairly insulated market, with most cosmetic surgery business forwarded by Bristol residents being retained by practices within the city.

To understand the competitive landscape further, Drs. Cook and Davidson decided to conduct field research in Bristol. Specifically, the two wanted to view each of the nine cosmetic surgery clinics in the city to get a better idea of their associated servicescapes. As both physicians were well known in Bristol, their investigations were limited by necessity to external drive-bys, permitting them to observe the state of each clinic's location, parking, and landscaping. But they were desirous of more detailed insights, which they would need to outsource to others who were unknown in Bristol and able to operate covertly.

In order to gain these detailed insights, Drs. Cook and Davidson looked to Samantha Jacobs and Dawn Webb, two nurses working with them in their current practice, both of whom they planned to hire when Northside Cosmetic Surgery Center opened for business. Samantha and Dawn were not known in Bristol, making them excellent candidates for undercover research.

Over a 2-week period, Samantha and Dawn were asked to conduct vehicle counts in the parking lots of all seven freestanding clinics at two points during the day—morning (between 10 AM and 11 AM) and afternoon (between 2 PM and 3 PM). Estimates were also sought for the medical center-based practices, although parking lot counts here were more difficult, making for less reliable indications of patient volume. Further, they were to schedule personal cosmetic surgery consults at each of the nine clinics for insights into ease of scheduling appointments, delays in being seen by providers, associated service delivery systems, elements of the servicescape, and so on. With this information, Drs. Cook and Davidson believed that they would possess everything that they needed in order to compile one of the most detailed of competitive assessments.

After intensive planning, Samantha and Dawn began their 2-week study, conducting the requested field research, including the observation and recording of vehicle volumes and the assessment of the accessibility of clinic locations. Further, their undercover marketing research led to highly detailed accounts of clinic operations, providing rough profiles of clients at each establishment, hours of operation information, clinical and administrative staff behaviors and service approaches, waiting room and examination room descriptions, and so on. Drs. Cook and Davidson assembled their own research findings, along with the findings of the nurses' research, into a competitive assessment report and felt very confident that they had perhaps the best insights possible, given the unusual efforts incorporated to examine the cosmetic surgery practices of Bristol. Without a doubt, the final report represented a treasure trove of information upon which the physicians could go about formulating competitive strategies.

Before proceeding to other aspects of the business plan, Drs. Cook and Davidson believed that it would be prudent to consult a business expert to ensure that their competitive assessment was on the mark. A patient of Dr. Davidson suggested that the two approach Dr. Maria Fernandez, a well-known marketing professor at Kingston State University. Drs. Cook and Davidson did so and Dr. Fernandez happily agreed to review the document, suggesting that the two visit her on campus for associated discussions.

After reviewing the competitive assessment, Dr. Fernandez highly praised the physicians for their efforts to understand direct competitors in Bristol, commenting that the insights gained from undercover surveillance efforts were most impressive. And while she viewed the report possibly to be capable of satisfying their bank's requirements, from the perspective of marketing planning, she viewed the work to be off the mark because of the report's omission of many competitive elements. Dumbfounded, the two physicians could not think of any other competitors in the marketplace. Dr. Fernandez then went on to explain what they were neglecting.

DISCUSSION

1. Dr. Fernandez surprised Drs. Cook and Davidson by indicating that their competitive assessment for Northside Cosmetic Surgery Center was incomplete. What elements of the assessment were missing? How might these competitive elements impact the operations of Northside Cosmetic Surgery Center?

2. Drs. Cook and Davidson directed Samantha Jacobs and Dawn Webb to go undercover to assess cosmetic surgery clinics in Bristol, with the two nurses even personally scheduling cosmetic surgery consults to gain competitive insights. What are your thoughts on the ethics of this approach? Why do you feel this way?

3. Although lacking formal training in business administration, Drs. Cook and Davidson sought insights from a business expert, but only after completing their competitive assessment for Northside Cosmetic Surgery Center. If the two physicians could restart the business planning process, given their lack of experience in the administrative sciences, what actions would you recommend and why?

4. Although the case provides some indications of associated requirements, investigate the competitive assessment process and prepare a step-by-step practitioner guide that could be used to carry out this activity. Select a local community with which you are familiar and, using the product of cosmetic surgery services, demonstrate how you would go about using this guide.

5. Assume that you are hired to lead Northside Cosmetic Surgery Center. What systems would you put into place to ensure that competition is continuously monitored?

CHAPTER 40

When a Rival Fails

SNAPSHOT

Institutions:
Cedar Valley Medical Center, a 515-bed, not-for-profit medical center providing general medical and surgical services
Trinity Hospital, a 470-bed, not-for-profit medical center providing general medical and surgical services
Trinity Health, a not-for-profit health system consisting of 35 medical centers

Location:
Burlington (population 256,231), located in the East South Central region of the United States

Character:
Leonard Jackson, President and Chief Executive Officer, Cedar Valley Medical Center

Context:
In this case, the top executive of a medical center ponders the effects of the impending closure of a competing establishment.

Leonard Jackson, President and Chief Executive Officer of Cedar Valley Medical Center, is facing the unknown. His medical center's longtime rival in the community, Trinity Hospital, will be closing in approximately 6 months as a result of a decision by its parent company, Trinity Health.

Trinity Hospital, which is located in the city of Burlington (population 256,231), has long been in financial distress, propped up only by funding provided by its parent company, which operates multiple hospitals in the East South Central region of the United States.

After many years of shoring up the institution financially, Trinity Health envisions no forthcoming improvements in performance and has decided to cease Trinity Hospital's operations. This matter is particularly troubling to Leonard, because Trinity Hospital is the only other comprehensive healthcare provider in Burlington. With its closure, Cedar Valley Medical Center will likely be overrun with patients, placing immense pressure on the establishment's resources.

Although Cedar Valley Medical Center holds the market leadership position, this has not always been the case. The fortunes of the two entities, in fact, have completely reversed over the course of three decades. Thirty years ago, Cedar Valley Medical Center was a simple general hospital, almost completely off of the radar for anyone seeking medical services. Trinity Hospital was in absolute control of the market and, as such, was on firm financial ground.

The sleepy Cedar Valley Medical Center, however, was about to be awakened with the arrival of Leonard, who saw potential where others did not. Despite its small size and virtually insignificant market share in the city of Burlington, Cedar Valley Medical Center was financially sound and possessed a dedicated governing board that, for some time, had been seeking a leader to foster growth and innovation across the institution. Their search came to an end when Leonard interviewed and presented his vision for the establishment. He was hired immediately.

Although other healthcare institutions offered much more attractive work environments and prestige, Leonard viewed Cedar Valley Medical Center as representing a blank canvas upon which he could craft a revitalized healthcare institution with enormous upside potential. He believed that with proper strategy and excellent execution, he could grow the establishment's patient base and he knew that he had the board's unconditional support to do so. He also was well aware that his growth efforts would go practically unnoticed by Trinity Hospital, which at the time, was suffering from complacency as a result of being the market leader for many years with few competitive threats.

Using the cloak of insignificance, Leonard slowly but methodically began to improve Cedar Valley Medical Center's product mix and servicescape.

Effective but highly economical physical plant improvements were made to shore up the appearance of the facility. Further, Leonard organized an initiative to recruit the best and brightest physicians to Cedar Valley Medical Center. This served to improve clinical operations overall, but it had the added effect of drawing each physician's established patient populations to the medical center, dramatically improving cash flow. Leonard also turned to advertising, a first for the institution, to heighten Cedar Valley Medical Center's awareness in the market.

Slowly but surely, Cedar Valley Medical Center emerged from obscurity. With the passage of a decade, the establishment looked completely different and began to represent a defined threat to Trinity Hospital's market dominance. Cedar Valley Medical Center had long outgrown its original facility, necessitating expansions which increased capacity and the opportunity for further market penetration. In 5 more years, market share was dead even between Cedar Valley Medical Center and Trinity Hospital, with Cedar Valley Medical Center overtaking Trinity Hospital's market leadership position shortly thereafter and extending the gap year after year to present day.

Despite many attempts in recent years by Trinity Hospital to retake the market leadership position, the establishment has never been able to regain its footing, a victim largely of Leonard's aggressive strategies and tactics. And while Leonard has provided strong, ongoing leadership at Cedar Valley Medical Center for 30 years, Trinity Hospital has endured a revolving door of management teams sent by its parent company in attempts to stem losses and regain share, with each effort being misguided, temporary, and ultimately in vain. Trinity Hospital indeed found the slippery slope of market share loss, culminating in its near-at-hand closure.

Leonard has enjoyed the spoils of war for many years, as he propelled the virtually unknown and unwanted Cedar Valley Medical Center into the prized position of market leader, but now he is faced with the realization that he perhaps might have been too aggressive and too successful. With Trinity Hospital's impending closure, the city of Burlington will lose 470 beds and a wealth of ancillary medical services. This undoubtedly will tax the resources of Cedar Valley Medical Center, as its 515-bed hospital operates generally at capacity, as does its complement of outpatient clinics and other medical resources.

Emergency medicine will shoulder an especially heavy burden as Trinity Hospital's closure will shut down the only other emergency department in the city. Once Cedar Valley Medical Center's emergency department capacity is reached, diversions to distant areas will be forced, potentially causing loss of lives which might otherwise be saved. Even for nonemergent services, the reduction of capacity in the area is problematic, because Burlington is located 70 miles away from the nearest urban area, further complicating out-of-market options for care delivery for the city's residents.

Leonard is worried for his institution, but also for the citizenry of Burlington, as Trinity Hospital's demise will have lasting ramifications, yielding a healthcare complex in the community incapable of addressing fully the medical wants and needs of the population. Trinity Health only recently announced its decision to cease operations in Burlington so much has yet to be determined. The impact of Trinity Hospital's impending closure will clearly spark the interest and attention of city leaders and state officials who will no doubt engage in discussions both with Trinity Hospital and Cedar Valley Medical Center.

Knowing of the closure's inevitable consequences for Cedar Valley Medical Center and the city of Burlington, Leonard has scheduled an upcoming meeting with his governing board and senior management team for the purpose of brainstorming on the matter. He believes that any difficult situation, any threat, or any challenge has the potential to be turned for the benefit of an innovative institution and Cedar Valley Medical Center is just that.

His intent during the brainstorming session is to identify as many scenarios as possible that might unfold over the coming months and plan strategies and tactics to address each possibility. Might Trinity Health seek a buyer for Trinity Hospital? If so, who might desire its purchase? Burlington? Cedar Valley Medical Center? An out-of-market health system? Private investors? What are the consequences of each of these scenarios?

What if Trinity Health simply seeks to liquidate Trinity Hospital, selling its component parts to the highest bidders? Should Cedar Valley Medical Center be proactive and seek to buy all or part of Trinity Hospital? These and other scenarios will be up for discussion and debate in this very important meeting.

DISCUSSION

1. With Trinity Hospital's impending closure, Leonard expressed that he felt as though his aggressive efforts at Cedar Valley Medical Center might have been too successful. In your opinion, is it possible to be too successful? Please be sure to justify your response.

2. Leonard proactively seeks to address the impending closure of Trinity Hospital by envisioning possible scenarios and planning associated responses to each situation. Although several possible scenarios are noted, think deeply on the case and develop a comprehensive list of possibilities. Then, indicate, in your opinion, the best and worst case scenarios for Cedar Valley Medical Center. Be sure to state your associated rationale.

3. Assume that Trinity Health approaches Cedar Valley Medical Center seeking to sell Trinity Hospital. Although the case does not provide specifics that would be required in evaluating the viability of the purchase, what things must Cedar Valley Medical Center consider in determining whether such an acquisition makes sense?

4. Trinity Hospital's decline was not immediate but instead had slowly been occurring over the years. With Trinity Hospital's closure being a possibility that would have revealed itself years earlier, what actions might Leonard have taken to proactively address this possibility before seeing it become a reality? What steps might have been in order for Cedar Valley Medical Center?

5. The case indicates that Trinity Hospital was once the market leader in Burlington, but that complacency resulting from its long-standing market leadership position and the lack of competition weakened the hospital's defenses, opening up opportunities for Leonard and Cedar Valley Medical Center to capture market share. What steps would you take to ensure that your organization does not fall into the complacency trap?

Glossary

Adoption Process   A series of progressive steps leading up to the purchase and consumption of new products.

Advertisement   A verbal and/or visual message, forwarded to others via paid mass media, that is designed to inform potential customers of product offerings and attract their patronage.

Advertising   A promotional method involving the paid use of mass media to deliver messages. Examples include newspaper, magazine, radio, television, and billboard advertisements.

Advertising Agency   An organization that exists for the purpose of developing and placing advertisements, and typically other forms of promotion, on behalf of paying clients.

Advocacy Advertising   Advertising that promotes a political, economic, social, or technological perspective of an entity, often calling for audiences to modify their behavior to adhere to given points of view.

All-You-Can-Afford Budgeting Method   An advertising budgeting method in which operational expenditures are identified and funded across given organizations, with the remaining resources (i.e., that which is left over after all other expenses have been paid) being assigned to fund advertising initiatives in the forthcoming period.

Antitrust Laws   Laws designed and developed to promote competition by forbidding monopolies.

Atmosphere   The aesthetic qualities of the environment of a particular establishment that combine to form an ambiance that has the ability to positively or negatively influence customers.

Audience   (1) The population that has been selected (i.e., targeted) by an organization for pursuit as customers. Also referred to as a target audience, target market, or target population. (2) The population that is exposed to a given mass media vehicle and is thus exposed to associated promotional messages.

Audience Fragmentation   A term used to characterize the dispersion of broad audiences resulting from the proliferation of various media sources that divide audiences into increasingly smaller groups, making it more difficult for marketers to conveniently reach target populations.

Availabilities   Units of advertising (e.g., space in outdoor advertising, air time in television advertising) that are available for purchase on a given date. In practice, the term is more commonly used in its abbreviated form—avails.

Bait and Switch Advertising   A form of deceptive advertising involving the promotion of a particular product, often at a very attractive price, as a means of generating customer traffic. When interested customers inquire about the advertised product, they are instead offered another item—typically carrying a higher price than the advertised offering—under the guise that the advertised product is of poor quality, has sold out, or is otherwise unavailable or inappropriate for their needs.

Barriers to Entry   Anything that blocks or otherwise prohibits an entity from entering and competing in a given market (e.g., regulations, capital requirements, superior competition).

Benchmarking   The practice of comparing the marketing performance of an organization and/or its product offerings to established standards of excellence known as benchmarks.

Billboard   A stationary advertising structure that is placed along transit pathways to display promotional messages to passersby.

Billboard Advertising   A form of outdoor advertising involving the use of stationary structures that are placed along transit pathways to display promotional messages to passersby. Standard billboard advertising products include the 8-Sheet Poster (6′ × 12′), the 30-Sheet Poster (12′3″ × 24′6″), and the Bulletin (10′6″ × 36′, 14′ × 48′, and other sizes).

Black Market   An illegal market that develops when goods and services are exchanged in violation of governmental restrictions prohibiting such transactions.

Brainstorming   An activity involving intensive discussion and thought regarding a particular matter of concern for the purpose of generating applicable ideas, solutions, and so on.

Brand   A name, logo, slogan, or other reference that identifies goods and services, thus allowing consumers to differentiate product offerings.

Brand Equity   The value of a brand.

Brand Extension   The application of an established product's brand name to a new product in an effort to capitalize on existing brand awareness.

Brand Loyalty   An intense commitment to a particular brand resulting from a customer's prior positive experiences with the given brand.

Brand Portfolio   The overall collection of brands held by an organization.

Branding   The process of developing, assigning, and managing names, logos, slogans, and other identifiers associated with products.

Buyer   (1) An individual who purchases a product either for his or her own use or on behalf of another party. (2) An individual who, as part of his or her formal employment duties, purchases designated products on behalf of an organization for use in accomplishing a given mission.

Call to Action   A request, forwarded by an advertisement, calling on audience members to respond in some desired manner (e.g., to purchase a product).

Cannibalism   The introduction of a product that either partially or completely serves as a substitute for an existing product held by the same organization, thus diminishing the sales associated with the existing item.

Caveat Emptor   A Latin phrase meaning "let the buyer beware," which serves to remind consumers of the need to investigate given products and the entities that provide them prior to completing a purchase in the marketplace.

Channel of Distribution   A pathway through which products are routed from their producers ultimately to the end users of associated offerings. This pathway can be direct, with products flowing directly from producer to consumer, or indirect, with products flowing from producer to consumer through one or more intermediaries (e.g., wholesalers, retailers).

Clutter   A term used to describe elements in the environment (e.g., competing advertising messages, distractions) that compete with the marketing communications of given establishments for the attention of target audiences. Also termed noise.

Cobranding   The practice of applying two brand names, each held by different organizations, to a given product offering in an effort to capitalize on the synergies afforded by combined brand identity.

Commercialization   The full-scale marketplace introduction of newly developed product offerings.

Communications Mix   The five promotional methods used by marketers to reach target audiences: advertising, personal selling, sales promotion, public relations, and direct marketing. Also referred to as the promotions mix.

Comparative Advertisement   An advertisement that presents the features and benefits of a product in relation to competitive offerings in an effort to demonstrate product superiority for the purpose of encouraging exchange.

Competitive Advantage   Anything possessed by an organization that gives it an edge over its competitors.

Competitive Parity Budgeting Method   An advertising budgeting method in which marketers estimate the level of funding that their competitors direct toward advertising and then fund their advertising budgets accordingly, essentially matching the advertising resources of their competitors.

Concept Testing   The practice of seeking consumer feedback regarding a hypothetical product offering or advertising message to gauge related interest and enthusiasm.

Continuity   An advertising scheduling strategy that involves the even, consistent delivery of advertising messages over an extended period of time.

Cooperative Advertising   An advertising arrangement in which two entities, often the retailer of a product and its manufacturer, agree to share the costs of given advertisements, yielding reduced per-entity advertising expenditures and increased sales that will be enjoyed by both parties.

Cost   The amount of money that entities must spend to produce and/or provide goods and services.

Cost Per Thousand (CPM)   A term, abbreviated CPM, which reflects the advertising costs necessary for a given advertising vehicle to reach an audience of 1000 individuals. The "M" in CPM represents the Roman numeral for 1000.

Customer   Any party (e.g., an individual consumer, an institution) that purchases the goods and services of a given entity. The party may or may not be the end user of the purchased items.

Customer Relationship Management (CRM)   A marketing practice involving the delivery of personalized attention, service, and support to target audiences in an effort to establish lasting bonds with customers, ensuring their enduring patronage.

Customer Satisfaction   A primary goal of any business entity resulting from successful efforts to meet and, ideally, exceed the wants and needs of customers.

Demarketing   A practice where marketers, notably in situations of scarcity, seek to lessen the demand for given product offerings by reducing or eliminating advertisements, discounts, and other purchase incentives.

Diffusion   A term used to describe the gradual acceptance of a new product in the marketplace that occurs over time.

Direct Marketing   A promotional method involving the delivery of messages directly to consumers. Examples include direct-mail marketing, telemarketing, and catalog marketing.

Distribution   All elements involved with making products available to target markets. Examples include the transportation of goods to retail establishments, the warehousing of finished products, and the determination of hours of operation. Sometimes used as an alternative term for the place aspect of the marketing mix.

Electronic Advertising Advertising that uses electronic media, notably including radio, television, and the Internet, to deliver promotional messages to target audiences.

Environmental Scanning An externally focused activity where marketers seek to assess the environment in an effort to identify marketplace trends.

Exchange A goal of marketing that involves the successful completion of a transaction between a buyer and a seller.

Flighting An advertising scheduling strategy that involves the intermittent delivery of advertising messages to target audiences. It is characterized by intensive bursts of advertising, which are preceded and followed by periods of hiatus.

Four Ps of Marketing The four interdependent components of product, price, place, and promotion that must be formulated for each product offering in an effort to attract target markets. Also known as the marketing mix.

Frequency A measure of advertising effectiveness that specifically refers to the total number of times that individuals are exposed to a particular advertisement. Frequency (i.e., the number of exposures per individual) and reach (i.e., the number of individuals exposed) largely determine advertising impact (i.e., the degree to which given advertisements are effective).

Good A tangible product offering.

Identity Management A marketing practice involving the comprehensive management of all elements related to the establishment and maintenance of institutional and/or product identity, notably including branding and advertising.

Impact A measure of the overall effectiveness of a given advertisement, which is largely determined by the reach (i.e., the number of individuals exposed) and frequency (i.e., the number of exposures per individual) achieved by the particular advertisement.

Integrated Marketing Communications The coordination of all of the marketing communications efforts of an organization for the purpose of ensuring the consistent presentation of promotional messages to target audiences.

Intermediary A participant in the process of routing goods and services from producers ultimately to the end users of associated product offerings. Also referred to as channel members, intermediaries include entities such as wholesalers and retailers.

Key Account A customer who is responsible for a substantial portion of the total sales of a given entity and thus warrants special attention from the associated organization.

Line Extension The addition of a new and typically related product offering to an existing array of products offered by an organization.

Macroenvironment External forces within the marketplace that, although beyond the control of executives, have the potential to influence organizations. Such forces are often divided into four categories: political, economic, social, and technological.

Magazine Advertising A form of print advertising that involves the use of magazines, typically circulated on a regular basis, to deliver promotional messages to target audiences.

Margin The difference between the cost of producing and/or providing a product and the price received for the given offering.

Market A broad collection of potential customers.

Market Leader The entity or product, depending on the focus of the assessment, that possesses the greatest share of a given market.

Market Penetration The degree to which a given product has acquired market share in a given market.

Market Potential The overall capability of a given market to deliver customers for a given product, with such potential ranging from positive to negative from the perspective of marketers who are responsible for promoting the designated product.

Market Segment A group of individuals within a market who share common characteristics (e.g., age, income, tastes, preferences).

Market Segmentation The process of dividing a market into groups (i.e., segments) of individuals who share common characteristics. Market segmentation is the first step of target marketing.

Market Share   An entity's portion, expressed as a percentage, of the total sales generated by a given product in a given market.

Marketing   A management process that involves the assessment of customer wants and needs, and the performance of all activities associated with the development, pricing, provision, and promotion of product solutions that satisfy those wants and needs.

Marketing Concept   A marketing philosophy, which became prevalent in the 1960s and remains so today, that recognizes and appreciates the valuable role of customers in marketing, leading marketers to focus their attention on meeting and exceeding the wants and needs of their target audiences.

Marketing Mix   The four interdependent components of product, price, place, and promotion that must be formulated for each product offering in an effort to attract target markets. Also known as the four Ps of marketing.

Marketing Plan   A formal document that describes and assesses the current marketing performance of an organization and sets marketing goals and objectives for the upcoming period.

Mass Marketing   The practice of offering products to the market as a whole without regard for the individual tastes and preferences of consumers.

Mass Media   A term that refers to the range of media vehicles (e.g., newspapers, magazines, radio, television, and billboards) that can be used to deliver promotional messages to large target audiences.

Microenvironment   Internal forces within an organization that have the potential to influence the given establishment. Such forces include capital, personnel, institutional capabilities, and so on.

Need   Something that is required for well-being and possibly survival. A necessity as opposed to a desire.

New Product Development   The creation of a new good or service usually resulting from a systematic process ranging from idea conception to commercialization.

New-to-the-World Product   A newly introduced product that defines an entirely new product category never before offered to the public.

Newspaper Advertising   A form of print advertising that involves the use of newspapers, typically circulated on a daily or weekly basis, to deliver promotional messages to target audiences.

Niche Marketing   A practice in which marketers target and intensively focus on fulfilling the wants and needs of a very defined segment of the market in an effort to serve that particular segment better than any other entity in the marketplace.

Noise   A term used to describe elements in the environment (e.g., competing advertising messages, distractions) that compete with the marketing communications of given establishments for the attention of target audiences. Also termed clutter.

Objective-and-Task Budgeting Method   An advertising budgeting method that involves the independent, ground-up development of an advertising budget based on the promotional wants and needs of an institution. Advertising objectives are identified, along with the tasks required to accomplish those objectives, and a budget is formulated accordingly.

Outdoor Advertising   Advertising that uses billboards, transit vehicles, street furniture, and other out-of-home media to deliver promotional messages to target audiences.

Outshopping   A practice in which consumers in a given marketplace forgo the goods and services offered by organizations in their particular community, choosing instead to purchase the products from other vendors in adjacent marketplaces.

Packaging   The exterior boxes, cartons, wrappers, and similar elements that are used to aid in the transportation of products to given sales locations and in the presentation of offerings to potential buyers.

Percentage-of-Sales Budgeting Method   An advertising budgeting method that calls for marketers to review sales for the previous period and determine an appropriate percentage that should be dedicated to advertising. The resulting amount then serves as the advertising budget for the forthcoming period.

Personal Selling   A promotional method involving the use of a sales force to convey messages to target audiences.

Place One of the four Ps of marketing, which involves the formulation of all elements associated with making products available to target markets. Examples include the transportation of goods to retail establishments, the warehousing of finished products, and the determination of hours of operation. Sometimes referred to as distribution.

Portfolio Analysis An activity involving the comprehensive review and assessment of an organization's product offerings.

Price (1) The amount of money that must be paid by customers to acquire particular goods and services. (2) One of the four Ps of marketing, which involves all elements associated with pricing products in a manner that will be attractive to target markets.

Print Advertising Advertising that uses print media, notably including newspapers and magazines, to deliver promotional messages to target audiences.

Product (1) Any offering provided by an entity for purchase and consumption. A product can be a good (i.e., a tangible item), a service (i.e., an intangible item), or a hybrid (i.e., an item with tangible and intangible characteristics). (2) One of the four Ps of marketing, which involves the development of goods and services that will meet and, ideally, exceed the wants and needs of target markets.

Product Class A collection of similar to diverse product offerings that serve related wants and needs (e.g., personal mobility—wheelchairs, walkers, and canes).

Product Deletion The elimination of a particular good or service from a given product portfolio.

Product Differentiation (1) The ability to distinguish goods and services from competitive offerings. (2) The development of distinguishable product features that allow offerings to easily be recognized by customers.

Product Form A particular manifestation of a product and its closely related variants (e.g., aspirin—regular, extra-strength, and P.M.).

Product Life Cycle A model that illustrates the four stages of a product's development: introduction, growth, maturity, and decline.

Product Portfolio   The overall collection of products held by an organization.

Product Positioning   The process of determining an appropriate and effective image for products to convey to customers in an effort to influence their perceptions of goods and services. Product positioning is the final step of target marketing.

Production Concept   A marketing philosophy, prevalent during the 1800s and early 1900s, that emphasized the production of goods and services, leading marketers to focus their attention on excellence in this area, typically at the expense of customers and their defined wants and needs.

Promotion   (1) All activities associated with communicating a product's attributes to target markets. (2) One of the four Ps of marketing, which involves the formulation of communications strategies and tactics that will effectively convey product attributes to target markets.

Promotions Mix   The five promotional methods used by marketers to reach target audiences: advertising, personal selling, sales promotion, public relations, and direct marketing. Also referred to as the communications mix.

Public Relations   A promotional method involving the use of publicity and other unpaid forms of promotion to deliver messages. Examples include press releases, open houses, facility tours, and educational seminars.

Pull Strategy   A marketing communications strategy that involves directing communicative efforts (e.g., advertising, sales promotion, direct marketing) toward consumers who, in turn, demand the associated products from establishments in the marketplace. Such activities essentially pull given products through channels of distribution, resulting in exchange.

Pulsing   An advertising scheduling strategy that involves the placement of a consistent but tempered number of advertising messages over a given campaign period, supplemented periodically by surges in the quantity of messages delivered to target audiences.

Push–Pull Strategy   A marketing communications strategy that involves directing communicative efforts (e.g., advertising, sales promotion, direct marketing) toward both intermediaries and consumers in the marketplace in an attempt to generate exchange.

Push Strategy   A marketing communications strategy that involves directing communicative efforts (e.g., advertising, personal selling, sales promotion, direct marketing) toward intermediaries who purchase the associated offerings and, in turn, promote them to their customers. Such activities essentially push given products through channels of distribution, resulting in exchange.

Radio Advertising   A form of electronic advertising that uses radio to deliver promotional messages to target audiences.

Rate Card   A document prepared by a media firm (e.g., a radio or television station, a newspaper or magazine publisher, an outdoor advertising plant operator) that lists various rates for given advertising purchases.

Reach   A measure of advertising effectiveness that specifically refers to the total number of individuals who are exposed to a particular advertisement. Reach (i.e., the number of individuals exposed) and frequency (i.e., the number of exposures per individual) largely determine advertising impact (i.e., the degree to which given advertisements are effective).

Relationship Marketing   A marketing practice involving the delivery of personalized attention, service, and support to target audiences in an effort to establish lasting bonds with customers, ensuring their enduring patronage.

Repositioning   The practice of altering the positioning characteristics of given product offerings in an effort to redefine the image associated with particular goods and services.

Retailer   An establishment that sells products directly to consumers.

Sales Concept   A marketing philosophy, prevalent during the mid-1900s, which emphasized salesmanship as a means of generating exchange, leading marketers to focus their attention on excellence in this area, typically at the expense of customers and their defined wants and needs.

Sales Promotion   A promotional method involving the use of incentives to stimulate customer interest. Examples include discount coupons, free gifts, samples, and contests.

Sales Representative   An individual employed by an organization to identify and contact customers in the marketplace who might have wants and needs for the goods and services offered by the employing establishment.

Segment   A group of individuals within a market who share common characteristics (e.g., age, income, tastes, preferences).

Segmentation   The process of dividing a market into groups (i.e., segments) of individuals who share common characteristics. Segmentation, also termed market segmentation, is the first step of target marketing.

Seller   Any party that offers products for sale to others.

Service   An intangible product offering.

Social Marketing   The use of marketing strategies and tactics to promote goods and services deemed to be beneficial to the health and well-being of individuals and society.

Substitute Product   A product that differs from a particular offering but largely, and sometimes completely, fills equivalent wants and needs. Laser vision correction, for example, could be viewed as a substitute for eyeglasses, with both products offering two different routes to better vision.

Supply Chain Management   A marketing practice involving the comprehensive management of distribution networks to ensure efficient and effective business operations that will ultimately yield goods and services of significant value.

Target Market   The name given to a market segment that has been selected (i.e., targeted) by an organization. Also referred to as a target audience or target population.

Target Marketing   A three-step process that involves the division of a market into segments (i.e., market segmentation), the selection of attractive segments to pursue (i.e., targeting), and the determination of an appropriate and effective image for products to convey to customers (i.e., product positioning).

Targeting   The selection of attractive market segments to pursue. Targeting is the second step of target marketing.

Television Advertising   A form of electronic advertising that uses television (e.g., broadcast network television, cable television) to deliver promotional messages to target audiences.

Test Marketing   A practice where marketers directly or indirectly seek consumer feedback regarding their new products by allowing target audiences to experience the offerings prior to full-scale marketplace introductions. Such experiences are offered to customers via product samples, trials, small-scale market releases, and other means.

Top-of-Mind Awareness   A marketing communications goal that refers to the first brands that come to mind when consumers think of products.

Transit Advertising   A form of outdoor advertising involving the use of public transportation vehicles (e.g., buses, taxis, trains) to display advertising messages to vehicular and pedestrian traffic in the course of their passenger transportation activities.

Unique Selling Proposition (USP)   A proposal forwarded to target audiences via an advertisement that touts the unique features and benefits possessed by a product offering for the purpose of attracting interest, attention, and exchange.

Value Added   A term that refers to the enhancements and improvements offered by given products that eclipse the features and benefits of current offerings in the market.

Vendor   Any party that carries a particular product offering and makes the item available to others for purchase and consumption.

Want   Something that is desired but not required for well-being and survival. A desire as opposed to a necessity.

Warehouse   (1) The act of storing goods for distribution or use at a later point in time. (2) A physical structure built for the purpose of storing goods for distribution or use at a later point in time.

Wearout   The tendency for the impact of an advertising message to diminish over time, necessitating that marketers periodically alter their advertising messages to ensure sustained impact.

Wholesaler   An intermediary in a channel of distribution that is situated between the producer of a product and the retailers that carry the particular offering.

Word-of-Mouth Publicity   Publicity generated via communications between and among peers regarding the benefits, or lack thereof, of given product offerings.

Zapping   A practice, undesirable to advertisers, in which television viewers use their remote controls to change channels during commercial breaks, thus avoiding exposure to advertisements.

Index